OVERD

a Cotswold affair

Cliff Hardy

Cliff. Hardy

High Street Publishers

Also by Cliff Hardy:
Farm, Forge, and Factory: the life of a village one hundred years ago

Published 1993 by High Street Publishers,
8 High Street, Lavenham, Sudbury, Suffolk

ISBN 0 9519811 1 0

Designed by Lois McCartney/Sally Jeffery Publication Design
Printed in England by The Lavenham Press

CONTENTS

Acknowledgements

I wish to record my thanks to the following people. To Pam, my wife, for it was she who encouraged me to press on with the task despite my reluctance at times to put pen to paper. To my son Paul and daughter-in-law Anne who showed great patience and affection in the days when my behaviour must have been quite beyond understanding. To Amanda Thornton for editing the book with considerable understanding and mature judgement. And to Sally Jeffery for producing the book to her consistently high standards and for her overall guidance with the project.

FOREWORD

Truth can often be stranger than fiction and if I had set out to produce the story in these pages from my imagination, I am convinced that the end result would have been far less interesting than the real story.

Eight years have elapsed since the events recorded here and I write of them now having had time to reflect on it all. My first feeling is one of extreme gratitude to the many friends whose concern for me became so apparent and who were so helpful. I have taken the liberty of mentioning many of them in this book and I hope nothing I have said will give any offence. I also made many new friends who are mentioned by name and I wish to place on record my appreciation for their help.

The story is an account of what happened when my instincts guided me to meet the challenge of buying and restoring a neglected cottage in the Cotswolds. It came at a point in my life when plans for retirement had been shattered by personal loss. As the narrative unfolds, incidents and situations are related which many readers will have experienced personally. The full flavour and atmosphere of the Cotswolds is apparent throughout and there are tastes of Scotland and Suffolk, the significance of which becomes clear as the story is revealed. Perhaps the book could serve as a guide for anyone undertaking a similar project and might even prompt others to consider embarking on such an adventure.

The story would not have been complete if I had concealed from my readers the account of my own personal relationships which are woven into the fabric of the book. To those involved I must say thank you for bringing me happiness in what would otherwise have been a time of despair.

I hope readers will find much in the book to entertain and amuse them for throughout the period there was much laughter at Overdale. It was for me an uplifting and enjoyable experience.

First sight

Chapter one

THE SEARCH

My first sight of Overdale was on a warm August afternoon in 1983 and I knew immediately that I wanted to possess the place. Occasions on which we feel so certain about anything are rare, particularly when we reach the age of maturity, but for me this was one. Looking back, the decision was quite irrational and most of the people who in time came to know what I intended to do felt the same. Many of them said so.

It seems that at the time I was not acting normally and it is possibly true to say that at almost any other time I would not have reacted as I did on that day, for by nature I am a fairly cautious person and make decisions only after careful thought. On that memorable afternoon I made a decision without taking account of any of the consequences and as time went by I produced a whole range of arguments to justify my decision. No one was able to persuade me to change my mind. I know now that their concern was for my welfare. They feared that living alone in what seemed to them a depressing environment of dereliction would be quite the wrong thing at that particular time.

I had no doubts about the correctness of what I was going to do and although I had many weeks in which to change my mind nothing could shake my belief in the future I had chosen. Indeed the more I thought about it the more my enthusiasm for the project grew.

When I first saw details of the property in the estate agent's window in Cheltenham I had a feeling that here was something I must investigate. I had gone to Cheltenham in the first place to attend a cricket festival. My native county of Yorkshire were playing Gloucestershire in a three day match interrupted on the Sunday by a one day game. This was an absolute feast (or festival) for me personally, for Boycott was at his best, showing us all the sides of his unrivalled technique. This was not the first time I had watched him at work during that summer, for I spent many days travelling the country to see Yorkshire playing, but specially to see one of the great batsmen of that time, the incomparable Geoffrey Boycott. He had his critics but no one could fail to recognise his consummate skill and tenacity. He had a special job to do and he always did it well.

An opening batsman has two objectives. The first is to lay the foundations of his team's innings and the second is to use his own individual skill in contributing significantly to the total score. The records prove beyond doubt that he accomplished these objectives time and time again, but it was the manner in which he did this which was important. He was the epitome of the highly skilled craftsman and I saw the full range of those skills during that summer. To understand the measure of his greatness one has to have a deep understanding of the subtleties and complexities of the game itself, for it can be just as interesting witnessing the duel between high class bowlers and leading batsmen as it is seeing a feast of run-getting. Boycott was a man for all seasons and of course, for all Yorkshire men, an idol of many years.

At Cheltenham he scored 140 not out in the three day game which Yorkshire lost, and 38 in the one day game which Yorkshire won in a most exciting finish. After this match Boycott was criticised by the Yorkshire Committee for his slow batting. Such criticism was unjustified and there were no complaints from those who watched his performance. The question must be asked, 'What about the rest of the team?' Perhaps if one or two had lasted longer at the crease more runs might have accrued.

My visit to Cheltenham was made even more pleasurable because I stayed three nights with Cynthia and Roy, both of whom were able to understand the experience I was going through since the death of my wife Doris in the spring of that year, for both had lost their partners. Cynthia had been married to Doris's brother Fred who died at the early age of 47 as a result of a heart attack.

At the time of my visit I was trying to come to terms with the death of Doris after 38 years of a very happy and fruitful marriage. What troubled me most was the fact that she had had to endure the pain and discomfort of her illness for so long and then go. This seemed so desperately unfair and there was so little that could be done to alleviate the suffering. In such circumstances we all do our best to bring comfort and support but it is all so woefully inadequate. Some ten years earlier we had suffered the loss of our daughter Anne as a result of a car accident and this had had a profound affect on us both. Carrying such a burden was not without its effect on the health of Doris.

My visit to Cheltenham and meeting Cynthia again brought back vivid memories of Doris's brother Fred whose untimely death brought great sadness to us all. I counted him as a true and very special friend. A man who had great potential and a most attractive personality; he had achieved much in his short life, interrupted by army service, much of it in the Italian campaign. Everything he undertook was accomplished to the very exacting standard which he set himself. I well remember seeing him only once on the football field. He was clearly playing in a class of football well below the standards he was accustomed to, but he brought grace and elegance to the match which was a joy to see, with not a trace of arrogance.

Some years earlier, as Fred lay in a Cheltenham hospital on what we thought at the time was the road to recovery, he wrote to us. I quote this letter in full as I believe it reveals the character of a very brave and special person, which no words of mine could ever do.

West Block
General Hospital
Tuesday 3rd

My Dear Doris and Cliff
You will be glad to hear from me I know, for it will immediately show that there has been a strong recovery and therefore no need for further anxiety. Blood pressure is still a little low and this will have to be improved before I can sit out any length of time. This is 'stop press news', the doctor was with me only an hour ago. I expect to sit out for an hour this afternoon. I have been sitting up in bed for the last two days but only this morning I was able to wash and shave myself.

Of course the drip has gone and so too now has the heart monitor. So I am now unfettered and much more comfortable, which also means that I sleep better at night, eat better during the day and generally feel cheerful.

You may have heard from Cynthia of the reversal we had last Thursday. A couple of shattering experiences. Walks in the darkness is perhaps the only way I can describe them and both times they managed to bring me back again, without a shred of dignity, and grovelling on the floor fighting for breath – but grateful.

Like I said a most devastating experience, no warning nor knowledge of anything until you're being picked up off the floor where they throw you for speed of treatment.

However every crisis has its other side. My heart had been out of rhythm since I had been admitted and it was one of the doctor's problems, how to correct it. They had in mind I now hear that I would be taken to theatre to have it stopped and re-started electrically. That proved not to be necessary after the two crises on Thursday. Since then everything has progressed with complete satisfaction.

Cynthia was fetched in on Thursday morning. The first one happened at 8.30am and she was with me poor dear when the second one happened at about 10.00am. She did not leave until 10.00pm and wanted to spend the next day with me. This did not prove possible or necessary.

I am happy you will be coming up next weekend and look forward to your visit now that the depression has lifted.

I have thought of you often since you went back and hope that you all may be settling down to a more normal life and that you are all well.

We have had many hours of sunshine and I am looking out over the College playing field and we have three vases of daffodils in the ward and they're such a lovely golden yellow in the sunlight.

From the Red Cross library I have just finished reading 'Akenfield' a portrait of a Suffolk village by Ronald Blythe. You may recall a BBC television extract of a short time ago where they interviewed some of the people who were written about in the book. Do try and get it through your library. I am sure you will both be enthralled with it as I was. Harry will call tomorrow and Reg on Thursday.

I look forward to seeing you both at the weekend.

My love to you all.

Affectionately
Fred

Not many days after this letter to us we had a phone call from Cynthia to tell us Fred had died. This was a bitter blow to us all and it was as though all the lights had gone out. We had lost someone who was irreplaceable. So much potential lost to us all and a man who showed so much concern for others, particularly for Doris and myself.

When I left Cynthia and Roy on the Tuesday morning on my way back home to Cambridge all these thoughts were on my mind, and I had a strange feeling that I needed to seek out something which might provide a challenge and an interest which would absorb me.

The Cotswolds held us in a spell for much of our married life. Doris was born there and for a number of years we lived and I worked within the area encompassed by Broadway, Winchcombe and Birdlip and our children were reared there. The ties were very strong and after spending four memorable days in Cheltenham, a town we knew and liked so much and with all the nostalgia that called forth, I saw no reason why I should not have a look to see what properties might be available; a small cottage in one of those lovely villages might well be the place where I should find something to fill the considerable void I felt from time to time.

Instead of taking the road to Andoversford, Stow-on-the-Wold and home, I decided to look round the estate agents in Cheltenham. Not far from the Theatre Royal, where several estate agents were situated, I browsed through the details of properties in the windows. Most of what I saw lowered my spirits slightly for as I expected they were mostly out of reach in terms of finance. One property however stood out in my mind from the rest, with the name of Overdale. It was situated in just the right place, a small village six miles from Cheltenham. The price still looked too high for me but as there was a note of unreality in the whole idea I thought I could at least get the details and have a preliminary look at the place.

At this point the whole thing might well have collapsed but for the fact that what I saw and read in the window gripped my interest. I went into the agents', where a young man was sitting at a desk at the back of the office. He seemed quite indifferent to my presence and I was about to approach him when a young man of similar type came through the door with something of a flourish and a roll of documents under his arm. He brushed past me and went up to the desk where he was given a warm greeting. This proved too much for me in my state of mind and I voiced my disapproval of the events. I said I strongly objected to the fact that someone who came in after me had been given prior attention. The young man at the desk did not take kindly to my approach and grudgingly instructed his secretary to find a copy of the details of Overdale. Having secured them I retreated hastily to the street vowing not to enter the building again and also saying to myself that should the property interest me I would in no circumstances purchase it through that particular agent.

A thorough examination of the details only made me more determined to look at the property which was on offer at around £47,000. I was sure that I ought not to be thinking of buying at that sort of price but now things were moving very fast in my mind and as a consequence I decided to get details of other properties on the market in the Cotswolds at lower values, in order to have some comparisons. I visited one or two other agents

The lane

where I was treated in a most civilised manner and managed to obtain five or six sets of details.

I visited one or two of these which were more or less on my way home, leaving Overdale in the village of Shipton Oliffe until last. The lower valued properties were interesting but none of them caught my imagination and finally I drove into Shipton Oliffe following the directions on the sheet, leaving the A40 at Andoversford and gently proceeding through the village. I was immediately captivated by what I could see of the village from the car. It was full of typical Cotswold cottages. I passed the tiny church on my right and drove up a gentle slope to the green. On the northern corner I spotted Overdale. This was obviously the place; a *For Sale* sign appeared in one of the bedroom windows.

I stepped out of the car and stood back to get an overall view of the property. This confirmed that my instincts had been right. It stood in its own grounds with a large garden at the back. I learned afterwards that there was other land adjoining which went with the cottage.

View from the front

Its appearance was indicative of neglect but not of decay. From what I could see by looking through the windows it was as most places would be if left empty for six months or more and the garden was on the verge of becoming a wilderness. The walls were sound and the roof was very good. It seemed to me to be in sound condition and so stoutly built that it would stand for hundreds of years.

I had no key and after about an hour of wandering around the garden and the lane in front, I became quite convinced that this was the place for me. I also noticed that the selling agents were not the same as the ones from which I had painfully obtained the details. Apart from my vow not to go back there it also pleased me to see other agents were involved. This normally indicates that finding a buyer has not been easy. I made a note of the agents' details and at that point decided to head for home in a high state of elation.

The details stated that offers around £47,000 were being sought. This gave me hope that it might just be possible to consider buying it and during

'Overdale', Shipton Oliffe, Cheltenham, Gloucestershire

Charming period detached Cotswold stone cottage, idyllic village position. Some renovation required.

Consisting of hall, sitting room, study/workshop, dining room, kitchen, bathroom, three bedrooms, good garden, store, outbuildings, garage space.

Price	Offers around £47,000. Freehold possession on completion.
Rates £221	Rateable value £172.
Services	Mains water, electricity, drainage to septic tank.
Accommodation	*Ground floor*
Entrance hall	Oak front door.
Lounge	(13' × 12' 6") Cotswold stone open fireplace, recessed display area with shelves.
Workshop	(13' 9" × 6') Suitable for conversion to study.
Bathroom	Shower cabinet, pedestal wash hand basin, low level W.C., ample room for installation of bath.
Dining room	(13' 3" × 11' 2") Attractive open brick fireplace, 2 windows with window seats.
Kitchen	(9' 9" × 7' 4") Range of modern fixtures comprising stainless-steel sink unit, base unit and worktops.
Conservatory area	Partly enclosed.
	First floor
Landing	Access to roof space.
Bedroom 1	(14' × 14' 8")
Bedroom 2	(12' × 10' 9")
Bedroom 3	(14' × 7' 6")

Garden

To the front a small area of garden with lawn, flower border and crazy-paved path. Opposite the front of the house is a triangular piece of ground formerly used as a vegetable garden. To the rear is a good-sized garden with large lawn and numerous flower borders. There is a small fishpond and rockery close to the house, and at the top of the garden, a greenhouse and small stone-built outhouse. Across the road to the west of the house is a stable.

A summary of the estate agent's details

my journey home, a distance of one hundred miles, I began to analyse the implications of leaving Eltisley and buying a cottage in the Cotswolds. Would it be possible to retain the house at Eltisley and also buy Overdale? What would be the point in having both? What about the financial implications?

I had now moved into a kind of dream world, but one which might be made to come true. It was all up to me and I could probably make it happen. The prospects, to say the least, were exciting.

Chapter two

THE DECISION

❦

On my return from the Cotswolds things might well have been gloomy, for it had been a wonderful four days but now almost by chance I had embraced a *big idea* which was to occupy my thoughts from morning till night for days on end.

I needed to tell someone about the find and as my son Paul and daughter-in-law Anne were on holiday in France I could not share my excitement with them. I went instead to see my neighbour who had been most helpful since the death of Doris. I visited her frequently and she was most generous with her hospitality. She was also a good listener and because of her own experience of losing her husband Michael, understood my own position. He was a helicopter pilot and had been killed instantly when his helicopter blew up and fell from the sky on a flight from Yorkshire to Cambridge. His death at such an early age had shocked the whole village, for he had become a much loved and respected member of the community.

Brenda had been left with two small children to care for and she had come through the most traumatic experience completely unaided and with considerable success. She had great strength of character and I much appreciated the help and advice she gave me. When she heard the news I got the impression that she thought the whole idea a trifle mad, to say the least, although she did not condemn it out of hand. She probably saw it as a sign of instability.

Having obtained the address of the other agent handling Overdale I telephoned their office the next day and was put through to the owner of the agency. He was a man of great charm and handled all my questions in a most polite and positive manner. He was the epitome of what a good estate agent should be and in sharp contrast to the one I had met the day before, face to face. He treated me as a person not simply as a possible buyer. I told him of my interest in Overdale and enquired about the asking price of £47,000. He was most helpful and advised me that he would put any reasonable offer to the owner. He said the place had been empty for a considerable time and that the owner was anxious to find a buyer. I assured him that I would be giving the matter some thought and would contact him again. Having got this far (and many of my readers will have gone through this experience) I was concerned in case anyone stepped in and took it from under my nose. I had to contain my impatience because although I could have proceeded, I felt a second opinion would be wise and this I intended to take from Paul and Anne. They were due back from a two-week holiday in France at the end of the week and so I had to wait two days for their return.

There was no problem in filling in the time for in addition to my domestic chores of washing clothes after my stay away, cooking and cleaning, there were many enquiries I had to make. Assuming I sold my Eltisley house, what would it be likely to make on the market? What if I needed a loan to bridge the gap between selling, and buying Overdale? What was the state of my own finances and what proportion was realisable? Getting a valuation on the Eltisley house could only be done on the basis of a serious intention to sell at some future date. This had to be the first step in a comprehensive enquiry.

The local agents were very efficient and promised to undertake a valuation within a few days. They fully appreciated that I might not sell in the end but were happy to proceed on the basis of my promise that if I did wish to sell they would be given instructions.

I then took stock of investments, savings and insurance policy values. What could I realise on them? What were the time factors in relation to insurance cover? And so on. All these facts must be known before I took any firm steps to purchase Overdale. I might also need to take up a long term loan and I would certainly need a short term or bridging loan in any case. Answers to some of these enquiries would take a few days to obtain and in the meantime I could concentrate on the next stage of my searchings.

With Paul and Anne due back very soon from their holiday, my intention was to telephone them after allowing them a little time to settle in after their return. One of the points I wanted to make was that my idea of moving was not influenced by the fact that they lived within easy distance of Overdale. I knew that as teachers they might well move at any time if promotion came their way.

Paul's reaction on the telephone was interesting. I had a feeling that he might think of my plan as being a bit on the wild side. In the event he expressed the view that if that was what I wanted to do I should go ahead and do it. He advised, however, that it might be wise to look at other properties before finally deciding about Overdale. This was a sound approach as it would enable me to check more carefully on property values and locations and to determine whether the choice of Overdale was too much influenced by emotional factors. He suggested that as they still had a few days before returning to work I should go and stay with them and they would come with me to explore other properties. I was much encouraged by their positive approach and looked forward with eager anticipation to my visit.

Next morning I locked up the house at Eltisley and set off again for the Cotswolds, grateful for the opportunity of sharing my ideas about the cottage with them and above all calling on their advice on what was an important decision. Apart from everything else I knew that I would be warmly received and that I would enjoy, as always, the splendid food prepared as usual to Anne's high standard. My own attempts at cooking had improved with practice but the meals had a certain amount of monotony about them. I was not disappointed. The meal was excellent and the wine (brought back with them from France) a fine accompaniment to the food. Our talk was first about their holiday which was quite naturally uppermost in their minds. They had spent two weeks in a rented farmhouse which had been a considerable disappointment to them. Apart from it not being as clean as one should expect, its nearness to the farm buildings gave rise to a fairly heavy infestation of flies. I got the feeling that some rather wet and cool weather did not help the situation. In summary it had been a good holiday in parts, but not one which they would wish to repeat.

Next morning we left the house well fortified by a full English breakfast and made straight for Overdale. Again we were only able to examine the property from the outside, but all the ground floor was viewable from the large number of windows.

It was difficult to gauge from their reactions what their real feelings about the cottage were but they did not condemn it out of hand. I think one of their concerns was whether the project of buying it and renovating it might prove to be too much for me to tackle at my age of 63. They also felt that the property might be overpriced, although they agreed that none of us were familiar with property values in the Cotswolds at that particular time. We knew that by and large values in these parts were well above the average.

The greenhouse

My second viewing of the cottage only increased my enthusiasm, for it was a place which possessed much character and although it lacked the quality of some, was full of interest. No two windows were alike, it contained two beamed fireplaces, each room was very different from each of the others and all contained interesting features. Nooks and crannies abounded and the largest room had a flagstone floor. The interior walls bulged and retreated in a most curious fashion and running through the downstairs area was a wide oak beam of early vintage.

Outside there was a garden rising from the house on three levels to an old outbuilding and greenhouse at the top some 30 yards away. The garden, although neglected, was full of interesting trees and shrubs. Three of the trees were apple and of considerable age. From the look of the fruit on the ground they had borne quite a crop. I was later to discover that within the boundaries of the whole property there were other fruit trees. In addition, raspberry and loganberry canes abounded. There was also a mass of gooseberry bushes of good quality. In the back garden near the house and almost overgrown we discovered a small waterfall which emptied into a small and very attractive pond, all in beautiful Cotswold stone.

Unknown to us at the time there was a well in the garden which later provided an item of considerable interest, and also two other pieces of land, one in front and the other at the side, each separated by a road. Both were large enough for use as building plots. Oblique reference was made to one of the plots on the original details but it was rather as an aside. In fact both plots were of considerable value, not least because they would prevent any

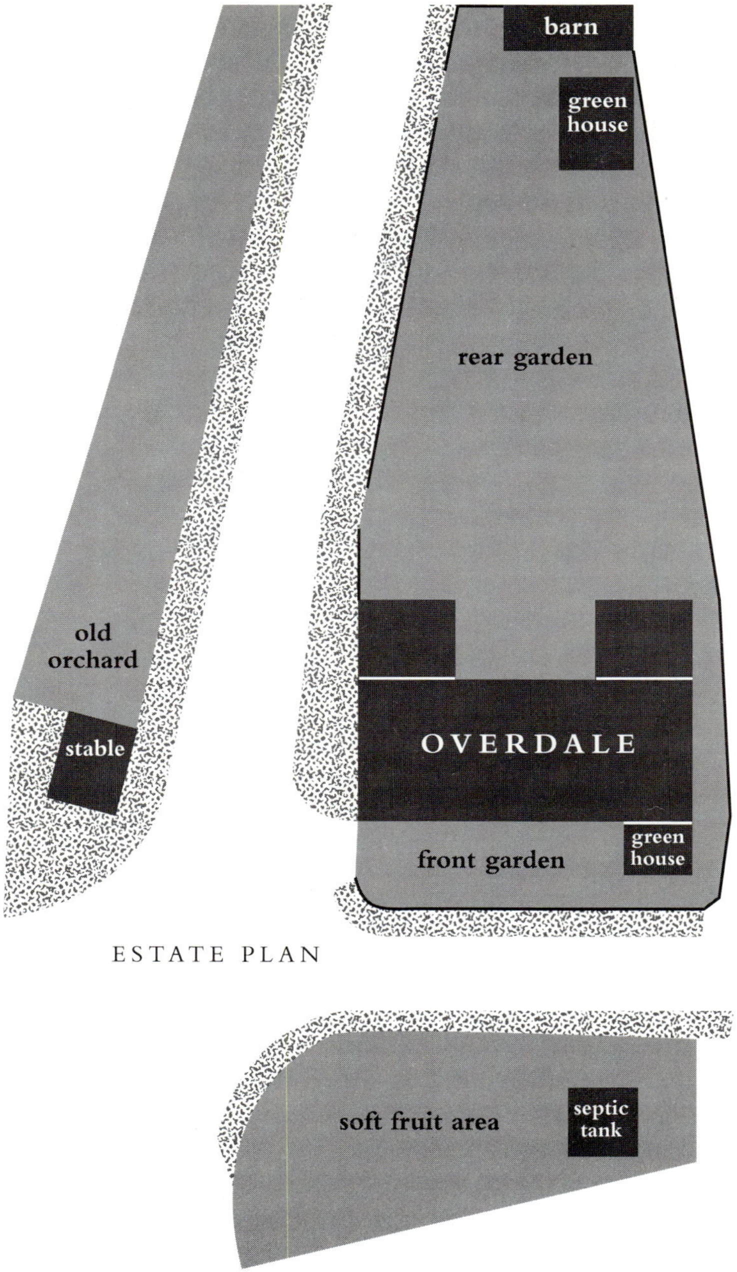

A plan of the house and land

The front orchard

other development obstructing what were outstanding views of the countryside surrounding the property. It is not often that one can buy a property and at the same time buy a guaranteed view. How many properties have been bought which have had uninterrupted views at the time and yet later the view is obliterated by some legitimate development? This could not happen to Overdale.

Having now taken full stock of Overdale we were in a position to conduct a search for similar properties in roughly the same price range of £30,000 to £45,000 and this developed into something of a marathon. We made a hurried dash to Stow-on-the-Wold, a good centre for the area. The old antipathetic feeling about estate agents began to creep up on me as I entered the office of one in Stow. I had had quite a bit of experience of these people and with notable exceptions they seemed to exude an air of superiority not found in other professions. I still find it difficult to understand why. For many years of course their job was easy for there were a lot of buyers and plenty of properties to sell. They themselves could not lose for they act as sellers with no risk, and each transaction gives them a fee. As I got to the counter my heart sank. The very superior lady who occupied the desk asked if she could help in a most casual manner. I immediately felt that she had made up her mind that their properties would be too good for me. This was underlined when she handed me a large tome which must have contained details of all the properties within a 100-mile radius, it was so big. She instructed me to look through the book and if there was anything I thought suitable, make a note of the number.

When I had noted those I felt might be suitable she would extract further details from the file. My enthusiasm faded rapidly for the system, which if I had used it to the full, would have taken me at least an hour. I handed the tome back to her saying that I did not have that sort of time. She was not amused.

The next call was much more rewarding. The girl at the desk knew what we were looking for and although some were slightly outside the price range, we had a stack of papers which proved very useful. We travelled on and it took on the appearance of a military operation. We drew up in front of houses on streets, in yards, across fields, down back alleys but found nothing which appealed. Many were overpriced and some were near to being unsaleable. We decided that we should need another day and also that we ought to try and get inside Overdale to have a proper look. The likeable agent was most co-operative and said he would be glad to meet us on site the following morning.

True to his word and in his inimitable charming way he opened the door and let us in. He was absolutely frank, pointing out the defects of the property, but also highlighting some of the good points of the place. As was to be expected it had been neglected since occupation had ceased and it was obvious that the occupants had been unable to care for it in the last period of their life there. It seems that the husband had been admitted to hospital and his poor wife had not been well enough to do much about the house. This presented me with no problems and in any case, I was viewing the place through rose-coloured spectacles. There seemed to be no problem which could not be solved, although some things like electrical rewiring would require a skilled person. Most other things I felt sure I could do myself. I certainly had a question mark in my mind about the damp in the walls but again I innocently thought that there was nothing that a good fire would not correct once the place was lived in.

I remember thinking at the time that once I got the place clean and some fires going there was little else I need do immediately, after all an aged couple had lived there quite happily for many years. I thanked the agent for his help and said I would be in touch with him again quite soon.

We left Overdale and started another sortie into the Cotswolds 'Country Cottage Market'. We looked at all shapes and sizes including one next door to a pub in the centre of a well-known village. It was a depressing place, cold and damp, and in any case I could not contemplate living so near a pub. Another one we saw had great appeal as we approached it from the front and it looked good inside. As we walked round the back into the garden we were met by a very strong smell of pigs and over the wall at the bottom of the garden we could see a massive piggery. It was nearing feeding time and the pigs were hungry. The noise from their squealing was quite penetrating. When I rang the agent to say that I was not interested in the property, he said 'Was it the pigs?' I was obliged to reply 'Yes' but in doing so I felt rather guilty. He had obviously got a problem in finding a pig-lover.

Another property, the details of which spoke in glowing terms about its desirability, was almost a ruin and worse in that it remained just as the occupants had left it on vacating. There were dirty pots on the table, dirty carpets on the floor, broken chairs and other debris scattered about. No attempt had been made to make it presentable for selling. In fact it remained empty for two years after we had seen it.

The last visit could have proved fatal to my idea about taking over Overdale. It was a lovely place looking onto a large village green. It was occupied and had been tastefully restored. It was slightly more expensive than Overdale and vacant possession would have been available quickly. I could have taken up residence there within a few weeks and nothing would have needed to have been done with the house for many years. In addition the carpets and curtains were to be included in the price and these were almost new and of top quality. Seeing all this made my decision about Overdale even easier. I needed a change, yes, but above all I needed a challenge. In any case there were so many interesting things about Overdale which appealed to me. It was bigger, it was located in a beautiful spot. The gentle slope on which it was built would afford protection from extreme weather and it looked out on to a lovely wooded valley. It had considerably more land attached to it, an old stable building, a greenhouse and a small stone-built low barn at the top of the garden. Above all it needed renovating for although it was structurally sound, there was much work to be done, some of which I could do myself both inside and out. This was the challenge I felt I needed.

We returned to Milton-under-Wychwood and over an evening meal discussed the events of the two days. Paul and Anne made it clear that they did not want to influence my decision but they felt that if it was my strong desire to buy Overdale I should take some firm steps towards that end or I might live to regret not doing anything about it.

I travelled home that night having decided to make an offer of £44,000 for Overdale. Paul and Anne had some doubts about such a figure securing the property which was on the market at £47,000 but in any case agreed that if this was my judgement I ought to proceed along those lines.

The next few days were full of anxiety. I had become so certain that I badly wanted to obtain Overdale that nothing else mattered. I rang the agent next morning as soon as I thought he would be in his office and informed him that I would like to buy Overdale at a price of £44,000 subject to a building survey. He did not suggest that this was too low, as I believe some agents would have done, and said that he would get back to me as soon as he had been able to contact the person concerned. Within two days he telephoned to say that the vendors had accepted my offer and that he would await confirmation of this when I had secured a survey. He also asked for the name of my solicitor. He obviously concluded that I seriously meant to proceed. I was naturally elated by this news and immediately took steps to deal with the matter of a builder's survey.

My plan was to seek the advice of a friend who was a foreman builder for a company whose main contracts were concerned with the renovation of old Cotswold stone properties. I knew he had all the expertise and experience necessary to undertake a general survey of the building. All I wished to know was whether there were any serious faults in the property which would be costly to deal with. My own feeling was, arising out of my experience of buying and selling houses (three in all), that if the walls were sound, the roof in good shape and the drainage system satisfactory, anything else would be of a minor nature. For example, I was well aware that the whole house needed new electrical wiring, but even that was functional, having been in use until relatively recently.

On the following Sunday I drove to Cheltenham having arranged with my friend to meet him at the cottage. I had managed to persuade Brenda and her daughter Sara to accompany me. It was a very pleasant autumn day and the Cotswold countryside was at its autumn best. The grey stone walls and the rich browns of autumn conspired to bring a magical touch to the place. All the ingredients were there to make it a wonderful day; the company of a female friend, the weather, and a closer examination of Overdale. In addition there was the added bonus of meeting Roger again after several years.

Having picked up the keys at Cheltenham we drove to Overdale, a short journey of five miles, and there to my delight I found that Roger was accompanied by his wife Rosemary, a person of whom I had always been very fond. After brief introductions all round Roger suggested that we get on with his inspection. He is a man of action and straight talking, and we set off round the house poking a window frame here and tapping a wall there, looking particularly hard at the foot of the walls. Shading his eyes he looked up to the chimney and roof, chattering away as he hurried along, but missing nothing in his inspection. Because the garden at the back sloped away from the cottage we were able to take a bird's eye view of the fabric of the roof. The doors at the back were in excellent condition as they were relatively new. The front door was of oak and very stout at that.

Once inside there was much evidence of damp and I wondered what Roger's reaction to this would be. Would he be horrified by what he saw? The previous owner had left all the floor covering down and so obviously I had not yet got round to even looking underneath. I did expect the worst. Roger hauled much of it up accompanied by a certain amount of snorting. I had seen for myself that most of the walls showed sure signs of damp and in fact one only had to feel them to accept that there was a problem. Roger's reaction was consistent with his whole attitude to the place. He had obviously seen it all before and it held no terrors for him.

All the downstairs rooms except the sitting room and the workshop had concrete floors. The workshop was a mosaic of stone slabs and concrete but the sitting room was paved with stone flags. This had the potential to make a showpiece when time was available to bring them back to their natural colour. Upstairs the wood floors appeared to be reasonably sound. In two rooms the floorboards were of a more recent period than the other rooms, where some reasonably good oak boarding was found. I say appeared reasonably sound but when I did occupy the cottage I discovered that some of them gave rise to problems.

The windows everywhere were in reasonable condition and the plumbing, such as it was, was good. There was a hot water system, heat being provided by an immersion heater. There was a shower room and washbasin downstairs, but no bathroom, washbasin or toilet upstairs.

Roger then went outside to explore the drainage system which was to a septic tank. There was a little hunt for a manhole cover which was buried under a mound of soil and plant life. He had the expert's instinct for finding where everything was. Access to the inspection pit having been secured, the drain was found to be extremely clean and the flow from all points in the house was good. Together we located the septic tank in the piece of ground over the road in front of the house. He lifted the inspection cover on the top of the tank and declared the system to be in excellent working

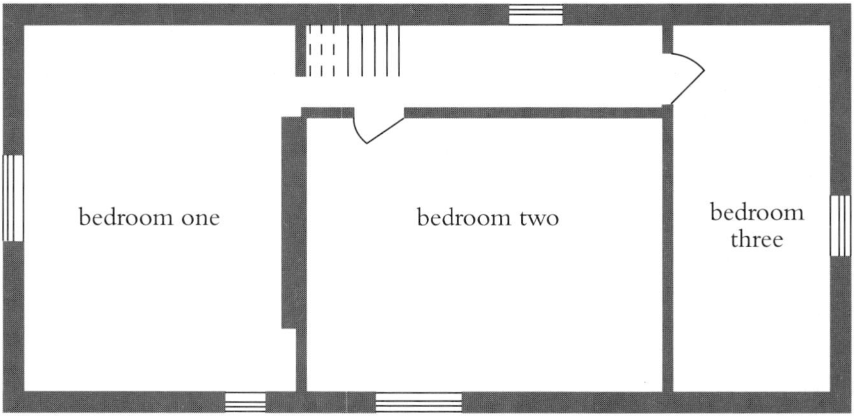

FIRST FLOOR

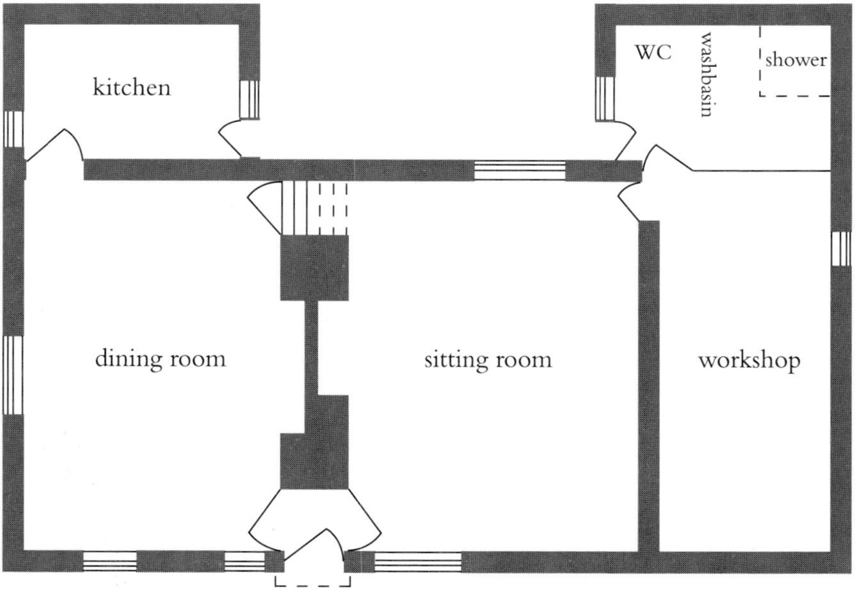

GROUND FLOOR

A floorplan of the house before work began

Rising damp

order. He pointed out a number of minor faults and problems, but of the damp he said that once the carpets were removed and fires were lit, the situation would improve, but in any case it could be cured by use of the injection system which was relatively cheap. Most of the other problems could be easily solved and many he felt I could do myself. On the positive side he asserted that as the walls were 24 inches thick and in good shape they would last for hundreds of years. The roof, which was of asbestos slates (quite in keeping with the Cotswold stone of the walls) was sound and of recent vintage. He informed me that he could tell from its shape that the timbers would be fairly new. He was quite emphatic that the cottage was a sound buy at the price and that with minimum work and expense would provide comfortable accommodation. It was a place on which a small amount could be spent to make it sound, or if sufficient money was available, it could be made into a most attractive and saleable property, the sort that was in great demand in that part of the country. He said it was a property that he would buy himself without hesitation if for some reason he needed to live in that locality.

He took his leave and I thanked him most warmly for sharing his expertise with me. At a stroke he had cleared away all the small anxieties I had that there might have been a major problem somewhere in the property which was not obvious to me. His robust and thorough inspection boosted my confidence and I now knew that I could proceed to purchase it with no lurking doubts.

The search was completed and the final decision made. I returned to Cambridge that night enveloped in a glow of real satisfaction and next morning confirmed in writing to the agent that my offer was now firm and I was instructing my solicitor to proceed with the purchase.

Chapter three

A SMALL MATTER OF FINANCE

❦

Having finally made the momentous decision that I would purchase Overdale, I now began to concentrate on how to make the dream a reality. Most people, and I would generally count myself amongst them, would explore the question of money before they embarked on the search for a property. In this case this consideration came last. It was likely to be the biggest financial deal I had ever embarked upon and yet it held no anxieties for me. I had convinced myself that the money could be found.

There was no question of being able to complete the sale of my Eltisley house before I would have to find the money to complete the purchase of Overdale, for now that the wheels of purchasing the cottage had started to turn the deposit money would soon be needed and not long afterwards the balance would have to be paid.

At this time the term *bridging loan* was very much in vogue. The housing market was quite buoyant and was being encouraged by the willingness of banks and other financial institutions to allow short term loans to those who needed money to buy a property before selling their own. Sure enough when I rang my bank manager in Bedford his response was very positive. He advised that we should meet at an early date and discuss the proposal. I was fortunate in that I held some insurance policies which were on the threshold of maturing and several other modest investments which could be realised. I also had insurance cover on a whole life basis and a further policy which had been held long enough to be used as security against a loan. I arranged a date with the manager and then, armed with details of my finances, I found my way to his office in Bedford.

This was a most pleasant encounter and I gained the distinct impression that he really hoped I would accept the terms of the bank's offer of a loan. Needless to say, I had no difficulty in persuading myself that I should go along with the idea. There were two reasons why I wished to secure a bridging loan: one which I have already mentioned was the time factor, to have the finance in readiness for purchasing Overdale before I had sold at Eltisley, and the other was a certain reluctance to leave Eltisley. I had established a very enjoyable relationship with my neighbour Brenda and female company was most important to me at this time. Brenda's attitude to me was most helpful. She had turned out to be a real friend in time of need. She had a remarkable sense of humour and was a very lively companion. Above all she understood me and was capable of sharing the experience of loss which was still very acute.

Such ambivalence in my attitude to moving was really something of a self-inflicted problem. Here I was, determined to buy a property in the Cotswolds and very excited about it, and at the same time anxious not to lose the companionship I had been fortunate in securing. I suppose I wanted the best of both worlds although I had no reason to believe that Brenda would be sorry if I left Eltisley. In fact with hindsight I think it was just possible at the time that I was a bit of a nuisance to her with my madcap ideas and unstable emotions.

The bank manager agreed that I should have a loan of £28,000 and my available savings were some £17,000. These two together would enable me to secure Overdale. My maturing insurance policies and investments which were to become available during the next six months would go much of the way to discharging the bulk of the loan. At the end of six months there would be an amount of £8,000 outstanding which I would clear by monthly payments of £220. The terms of the loan were 5 per cent interest over the banks' base rate and the loan could extend over a period of 69 months. I had to agree that as security, the bank had a first legal charge on my Eltisley property and charge over my life insurance cover of £22,000. Both these conditions were easily acceptable for I had responsibility to no one but myself.

The whole process seemed so simple that I found it difficult to believe that it was happening. Here I was asking for £28,000 and it seemed as easy as buying a shirt or tie. It has to be remembered that this was the time when properties were steadily increasing in value at about two or three per cent each year and in a way I was getting the loan for next to nothing. Both the properties, my house at Eltisley and my new acquisition in the Cotswolds, would become more and more valuable over time so that in effect I could not possibly lose out. All of this was in stark contrast to what is happening today (1992) when property values are falling year by year.

I realised of course that given the state of the cottage I would need to spend money on its restoration but this could proceed slowly as and when I could afford it. In any case I had a small reserve of savings to make a start. In addition I held a credit card with a substantial sum available as a back up. Fortunately my home was very saleable and could be on the market and sold within a few weeks of a decision. This was according to the local estate agent who had the property on his books.

The whole operation took on the aura of an enormous adventure. I was suddenly a man of property adding a second establishment to my assets with spare money and sufficient security to do almost as I wished, particularly with Overdale.

The feelings of elation I had at the prospects ahead were engendered by the fact that I was putting no one else at risk. If for any reason things went wrong I would have to carry the can and dig myself out of trouble. In any case the finances were so sound that the margin of error was very small. Taking the worst scenario – if anything happened to me – there would be ample money available to meet all commitments and a reasonable sum to spare for passing on, all of which would have been handled by my solicitor with no problems to anyone else.

I could now rest content that the securing of Overdale was a mere legal formality and in the capable hands of a very good solicitor. He was a personal friend who I knew would set the wheels in motion to allow possession at the earliest possible date.

I am sure that Brenda was aware of my feelings of elation and that I was beginning to shed some of the sombre moods which overtook me at times. I certainly found happiness in her company and tried in my way to show some gratitude for all her kindnesses. We had enjoyable trips to the Arts Theatre at Cambridge, and occasionally we would spend an hour or two in a cosy pub in the next village. Brenda's two teenage daughters gave me the impression that they did not mind my frequent visits to their home although looking back now they may very well have thought that I was an intruder on their family circle. They did not show it, if they felt it, and this gives me good reason for being grateful to them for showing such tolerance.

So life was very full. The Overdale saga was beginning and in addition to my good relationship with Brenda I had a wide circle of friends whose care and kindness was overwhelming. In particular David and Mary went out of their way to help me through the time of grieving. David, who is a consultant at the Cambridge hospital where Doris spent the last weeks of her life, was a tower of strength throughout that time and for a long time afterwards. They both visited Doris regularly and I know brought great comfort to her. They were both committed Christians and were active in the life of our local parish. They lived as they believed and despite my own unwillingness to accept their beliefs, they treated me as a true friend. They were generous to me in their care and concern and went out of their way to share their home and family life with me. In their company and in their home I felt a sense of warmth and peace which was rare. I owe them a debt of gratitude which I will never be able to repay. If heaven has any reality they will in due time undoubtedly be there. At the memorial service to Doris in our little village church, David read the lesson and some days later I was told by a friend who was a man not given much to emotion or sentiment, that he had never in the whole of his life heard a bible reading which moved him to tears. He said it was like a revelation and it was undoubtedly a most moving experience. My abiding impression of Mary is one of gentleness and concern for others. To complete this portrait, inadequate as it is, I must also add that they both have a great sense of humour. There was much laughter in their home in which I could share freely.

As I write, other people come readily to mind and in particular Mrs Vera Meeks, a near neighbour. For years she had been a true neighbour and friend, always anxious to help when trouble came. She conveyed a real sense of affection for Doris and me and I know that she and her late husband shared our grief a long time after the death of our daughter Anne. During the latter part of Doris's illness she was a constant visitor bringing warmth and cheer and often practical help when it was most needed. Her husband was a gifted cricketer in his day and he and Vera held Geoff Boycott in high regard.

Michael and Inez Cropley were also a great help to me and their home was an ever open door and a place where I really felt at home. We had a most easy relationship and much in common. Michael and I served on the Parish Council together and when work was to be done, especially of a practical nature, we would be found working very happily together. We had an instinctive understanding of each other which enabled us to form an effective team. In addition to a multitude of attributes Inez was an excellent cook and I frequently benefited from their generously laden table.

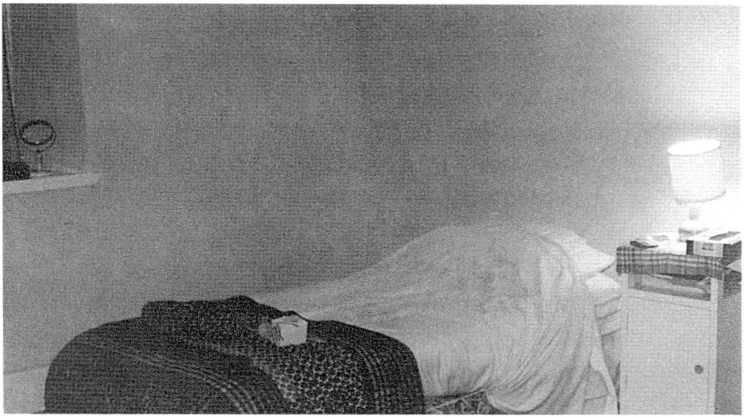

Camping out

As so it was, that despite all the attractions of the Overdale project, there was a plethora of reasons why I should stay at Eltisley. I found a temporary solution by making brief visits to the Cotswolds and on returning home continuing my social round interspersed by the domestic duties that I had sworn to do thoroughly. There was cleaning to be done, washing and cooking, and above all the tending of the garden which Doris had spent so much time in establishing. I was quite determined that nothing should be neglected in the house and that the garden should be maintained at the high standard set by Doris. I found working in the garden a source of solace. This I believe came from the fact that we had worked at it together and it held so many happy memories of the joys we had shared.

I was also developing my cooking skills. I saw no reason to live like some itinerant hermit and I gradually increased my repertoire of dishes. There was ample guidance to be found in the cookery books which Doris had assembled over time and I found that by carefully following the recipes I could make a very tolerable meal. I had two main dishes initially, both of which I found simple to produce and which seemed to meet all my nutritional needs. One was beef casserole, an easy dish which could be left to cook whilst other things were being done and in which one could ring the changes by adding different root vegetables. It was free of disasters provided one followed the most elementary rules. Additionally one could make enough to serve for a second meal the following day or the one after that. All my life I have found rice pudding to be a most acceptable sweet course and as tinned rice pudding is one product which cannot be adulterated, I kept by me a constant supply. My other speciality was toad-in-the-hole, a well-balanced dish of sausages and Yorkshire pudding. I consumed great chunks of it and my mouth waters even now at the though of it.

So I waited somewhat impatiently to get possession of Overdale. On my short visits there I at first stayed with Paul and Anne and although I was not legally entitled to set foot inside the property I nonetheless did get unofficial access for there were two sets of keys, one held by the agent and one by me in order that I could undertake the survey as described in the previous chapter. I persuaded myself into the belief that it was perfectly legitimate to enter the property provided that I did nothing to harm it. It did not seem sensible to waste time on legal niceties, after all I had access to the necessary money and the sale had been agreed and documents were being drafted. After my first visit I became increasingly bold until eventually I persuaded myself that I might start camping in the house. I suppose technically I became a squatter.

At this particular juncture I began to entertain ideas about using Overdale as a source of income instead of as a second home. I suspect that subconsciously I believed I might opt to stay at Eltisley for longer than I had at first intended and this was a way of turning the situation to profit. Placed as it was in the centre of some of the most beautiful countryside in England within easy reach of some of the most famous towns and villages in the Cotswolds, it was obviously very marketable. Cheltenham Spa was only 6 miles away, exotic places like Stow-on-the-Wold, Bourton-on-the-Water and Chipping Camden were only 30 minutes' drive away, not to mention Broadway and Stratford-upon-Avon. I had visions of the wording I would use in advertising this Cotswold stone cottage standing in its own grounds in the peaceful village of Shipton Oliffe. Who could resist such a place?

There were some problems of course, for it would need someone on the spot to deal with the changeover from one set of tenants to another. Could this be something which might interest Paul and Anne who lived 16 miles from Overdale? I did not envisage that they would need to do the work involved in the changeover but rather to manage the operation and be available if necessary to see that it took place without hitches. I was certain that the enterprise could generate sufficient income to allow us to employ a lady in the village to deal with the cleaning, etc., if such a person could be found. My plan would be that we would take half shares of the profit on the enterprise.

On my next visit I raised these ideas with them with a certain amount of trepidation as I knew that at the time I was not so cautious in my approach to new ideas as they were. What I saw as a mutually profitable concept may have seemed to them an intrusion into their well-established lifestyle. Their first reaction was not unfavourable although I think they regarded it with a measure of amusement. Above all I imagine they wondered why it was that after all my initial enthusiasm I was now pulling back from my intention to leave Eltisley. They agreed to think about the proposals in principle and to give me an answer in due course.

After about a week they told me that they would be glad to join in the enterprise and I suggested that we should have an early meeting to hammer out the details and the implications of the plan. I was now in a new situation. Overdale must be prepared as quickly as possible for occupation by holidaymakers for there would only be a limited number of weeks left to let the cottage in the holiday season. We did agree however that the place would have an attraction to many people even in the winter. The prospects ahead were even more exciting. I could continue to maintain my relationships in and around Eltisley, I could develop Overdale as a holiday centre and share the project with Paul and Anne. I was now gripped with a sense of urgency which I welcomed. This was no time for waiting about for things to happen but a time for action.

Chapter four

ILLEGAL OCCUPATION

Now that a decision had been made about what to do with Overdale I was determined to waste no time. Much needed to be done before we could open up for holiday visitors and it was pointless delaying the start of the cleaning up process even though as yet contracts had not been signed. This was the essential first step and would allow me to make an assessment about what needed to be done in phase one of the operation.

I had a strong desire to physically occupy the place by putting a bed and a few essentials into it so that I could camp there for short periods, but after some thought I decided to delay doing this until I could be assured that the purchase would be 90 per cent certain. In the light of this, visits were limited to a few weekends when I stayed overnight with Paul and Anne. The first of such visits was spent undertaking a survey in order to decide what the priorities should be and, without doubt, the question of rising damp was paramount. Roger had pointed out that if the floor covering was taken up throughout the ground floor there would be an immediate benefit as the floors would then be able to breathe. I am sure he was absolutely right but I felt that as the carpets were in reasonable condition, I should retain them for the time being but in the meantime roll them away from the periphery of each room during the period when I was away from the place, and as a result undoubtedly some benefit did accrue.

There were several places at the foot of the outside walls of the house where soil had been built up for flower beds, etc. These were clearly adding to the problem of damp, and clearing these was a job which could not be delayed so I made a start on my first visit. Two other factors stood out. I needed to secure estimates for dealing with the damp problem which was virtually everywhere on the ground floor and, as soon as possible, I must introduce some form of heating. We were well into October and the place was getting colder and colder. The only source of heating consisted of two pathetic electric fires of unknown vintage which were so small and ineffective as to be useless. These appeared to have been the only source of heat used by the aged couple who had previously occupied the cottage. Their generation were much hardier than we are and seemed better able to cope with the cold than we can.

In the sitting room there was an open fireplace with a most unusually-shaped bressummer beam. The fireplace had been modified in two stages, presumably to make it smaller and achieve an economy of fuel consumption. The end result was quite unique but no doubt it did have the effect of reducing the size of the fire and of the smoke exit. The final modification appeared to have been done to accommodate the three-bar electric fire which still occupied the space. Previously there had been a small firegrate in the space, which I found later in the stable outhouse.

The electric fire, apart from being totally ineffective, was positively lethal. The lead from the plug, which was a round three-pin variety, had the appearance of having been attacked by mice. Most of the electrical installations throughout the house were well past their 'sell by date' and would have sent the Electricity Board's officers into paroxysms of rage. This is a separate story to which I shall return in another chapter.

I had been thinking that the ideal solution to the heating problem would be the installation of a central heating system but to do that at this stage was quite out of the question. Woodburning stoves were all the rage at this time and were almost synonymous with country cottages. Until you had installed a woodburner you had not arrived. Furthermore I believed that such an installation was compatible with central heating; indeed there were some which could also be incorporated into the central heating system as the water heating unit. So, it would be a woodburning stove and the quicker the better. I took the dimensions of the fireplace in readiness for my search.

In addition to the question of the heating I came to the conclusion that I must explore the issue of damp proofing in all downstairs rooms for they were all showing signs of damp, particularly the outside walls. The kitchen was worst of all and there was no doubt that this needed early and drastic attention. The walls had been clad with hardboard to window level and this was beginning to rot at the bottom. This was to be expected because the kitchen, added to the main building at some stage, had been built into the bank. The roof met the wall only a foot above ground level. In other words the back wall of the kitchen was buried in the earth as if it were a foundation.

The Little Wenlock

There was no way that damp could be eliminated from the wall save by a major excavation. As this was out of the question, all that could be done was to render the wall as impervious as possible to keep the damp outside.

During that weekend Paul and Anne came to visit me at the cottage and helped with one or two cleaning tasks and we returned to their home on Sunday evening. They endorsed my idea about a heating unit and they also undertook to contact companies who might give an estimate for the damp-proofing work.

I returned to Overdale on Monday morning, calling at Burford on the way. My first encounter with the concept of woodburning stoves had been in a shop in Burford some years earlier. The shop was still in business and they had clearly gone from strength to strength in the field of fires, for the shop was full of heating units of all shapes and sizes, some of them large enough to heat a large hall and going down the scale to those which would fit into a small cottage. I would imagine that there are more woodburning stoves to the acre in the Cotswolds than anywhere in England and this shop had developed to meet this need. It was also gratifying to find that they really knew what they were talking about. I was quite inexperienced but unlike some unscrupulous salesmen whom we have all met, they were keen that I should have exactly the right model. In my ignorance I could easily have bought a stove which was too big or too small. We quickly narrowed down the choice to two stoves, either of which would meet my requirements on performance. I eventually selected a small multi-fuel Coalbrookdale stove known as The Little Wenlock which I believed would look good

The stable

in the context of the Overdale sitting room. It was of traditional design, very plain but obviously very functional. It came out of a very good stable from a company which had cultivated stove making into an art form and it came from a centre of traditional iron manufacturing famous throughout the world. In due course The Little Wenlock became the envy of almost everyone who came to the house. The Coalbrookdale Company had been established in Shropshire in 1709 and the story of their record in producing a range of products since that time is an epic. I knew I had chosen well.

The stove cost £215 plus 5 per cent VAT, the chimney lining £13 and the fitting of the stove, which the shop would arrange, would cost £50. I was warned to have the chimney swept before fitting so that I started with a soot free situation. I could not wait for the fitting to take place.

I returned to Eltisley that evening feeling that real progress was being made. I also had an interesting week ahead. On Wednesday evening I had been invited to a meal with Pam, an old friend and colleague, who lived at Glemsford in Suffolk. It was almost a year since we had last met on the occasion of our retirement from service with the Agricultural Training Board. Pam had been in Australia when Doris died and was quite unaware of my situation for some time after her return. As soon as she heard she wrote to me offering condolences and inviting me to a meal. After some time we had found a mutually suitable date and this was it. We spent a very pleasant evening together. The food was good and the drink, although not excessive, combined to make a most enjoyable evening. I probably talked too much (not unusual) but a lot had happened to us both and there was a lot of catching up to do. In any case this was a new experience for both of us, for all our previous meetings had been in the context of work. Pam was, and still is, a good listener and amongst other things I mentioned my friendship with Brenda and how helpful she had been. She thought that it was good for me to be able to share my problems with someone who had such understanding.

As I travelled home I thought long and hard about my relationship with Brenda. She understood me and had been kind and helpful at a time when I really needed help. I began to think however that my hopes of the relationship developing further were likely to go unfulfilled. I had no doubt that she regarded me as a good friend but there were a host of good reasons why she might not wish to become too involved with me, not least the question of my age. I came to the conclusion that time might resolve the matter. In the meantime I would take each day as it came. I spent the following evening with Brenda and needless to say it was immensely enjoyable.

Life was so full that the keeping of a diary was absolutely essential if I was to avoid the danger of needing to be in two places at the same time or of letting someone down by being unable to meet them. I also used it to record the details of all the activities and materials concerned with the work at Overdale. One thing which interested me amongst so many others was the cost of electricity which was being consumed at this time. I was not the legal owner but I was using electricity and I knew that it was important that at some point I must make payment for it. I therefore kept a regular record of meter readings. The other reason was that I wanted to know what the running of the house on electricity was costing. This would allow me to make comparisons when I made changes in the system as I intended to.

On 26th October 1983 I had a letter from my solicitor saying that he required £39,000 in order to complete the purchase of Overdale. I had sent my cheque for the initial deposit of £5,000 some weeks earlier. It was clear that things were moving rapidly now and that my illegal occupation was becoming less and less serious.

Almost at the eleventh hour a rather unpleasant happening took place. I was at Overdale and as on other occasions, doing some basic cleaning when the front door bell rang. I went to the door to be confronted by a lady of about my age and a younger person who turned out to be her daughter. It became clear that the lady was extremely irritated and wanted to know who I was. I told her that I was the purchaser of the property. She then went on to say that I had no right to be on the premises. She announced that she was an executor of the deceased owner and as far as she was concerned my action was not acceptable. Her grounds were that the sale had not been completed. In an attempt to pacify her I said that I had been informed that the contracts had been exchanged and that the purchase money was in the hands of my solicitor. I also made the point that I could still withdraw from the sale if that was her wish. My remark seemed to put the matter into perspective and she then became quite helpful. I did understand her position and of course, she was quite justified in pointing out the error of my ways. On the other hand I did feel that the few tasks I had undertaken to date had done nothing to devalue the property but rather that they had added value. The place was now much cleaner and more presentable for selling.

We parted on excellent terms, she undertaking to clear the house before the date of handing over. In the event this promise was partially kept although as with most other transfers of ownership, there were still quite a number of items left about. I did assure her that I would deal with these.

Before leaving she gave me a potted history of Overdale, saying that there was a gravestone in the front garden of the house on which the name of Geggs was just discernible. It seems that this family had occupied the cottage over several generations until they bought it in 1800. The record in the Gloucestershire archives shows that in 1800 many cottages in Shipton Oliffe were sold for £50 and because Overdale was then divided into two separate cottages, the Geggs paid £100. Traces of the stairway of the second cottage were still visible. The room, integral to the house, which had been used by the owner as a workshop, had once been known as the cellar. The place had the feel of a cellar as it contained only a tiny window and at one end there was an alcove shelf suitable for holding a barrel of beer. The cellar was also used as a place for hanging sides of bacon during the curing process. She confirmed my belief that both of the downstairs rooms had boasted an open beamed fireplace and claimed that in their original state they were big enough to allow access and that part way up the chimney there was an iron rod used to hang the bacon on for smoking. She also affirmed that the firebaskets for both fires were in the stable.

My interest had been aroused by some hooks protruding from the ceiling in the sitting room and she convinced me that these would have been used for hanging the hams of the domestic pig, a common enough practice in rural areas many years ago. She drew my attention to a stone set into the steps which led from the back of the house up into the garden area. This was part of a gravestone upon which was a faint trace of the name Geggs, another piece of evidence about the one-time occupants. It was, to say the least, rather strange to find that a gravestone had been put to so profane a use.

To further enhance the picture, she described how at one period the cottage was occupied by a cobbler who travelled around the countryside in a horse and trap, picking up boots and shoes for repair back at Overdale. It seemed that part of the dining room had been separated off to form a shop where local customers would bring in their footwear for attention. There were traces of marks on the ceiling which added weight to this idea. There was no doubt either about the stone outbuilding across the road from the corner of the house having been used as a stable, for on examination I found the remains of a stall in a reasonable state of preservation along with small items connected with the keeping of a horse.

Although our encounter had started on rather a low note, the lady's visit had turned out, from my point of view, to be a very fruitful one. It had the effect of encouraging my belief that Overdale was going to prove to be an even more interesting place than I had at first realised. There was clearly a lot to be explored in and around the house and I was moving rapidly to the moment when I would have complete possession of the place and to a point where real exploration could begin. My solicitor had promised to pursue the matter with urgency and, true to his promise, he telephoned me on 7th November to say that he now held the title deeds of Overdale. It was a wonderful feeling that at last I could enter the property and feel that I could do exactly what I liked. The time for real action had arrived.

Chapter five

THE HOLIDAY COTTAGE

Although my visits to Overdale before I obtained the deeds had been full of excitement, there was always a note of unreality about them for, despite my boldness in entering the place illegally, I was inhibited from doing anything of real significance other than tinkering with cleaning and tidying up the place. Now it was all for real and action had to follow quickly, particularly as the plan to prepare it ready for use as a holiday cottage must be put in hand immediately.

I had to decide what needed to be done as a matter of urgency and what could be left; what, in other words, was essential to make it habitable and what could be left for the long term. As we were now in November an improved system of heating was absolutely paramount. There was no gas in the village and everything in the cottage was electrical, some of it, as already mentioned, quite dangerous and not to be retained. The hot water system served by an immersion heater was quite functional as was the electrically heated shower unit. The wall heater in the shower room was fairly new and although far from luxurious was adequate, as was the wall heater in the kitchen.

The installation of the woodburning stove in the sitting room and a large electrical heater for the dining room would complete the heating requirements and so I made contact with a chimney sweep who agreed to come the following day, 9th November. I then contacted the shop in Burford who agreed to deliver the woodburning stove the day following the visit of the sweep. They had also obligingly arranged for the stove fitter to come on the morning of the delivery day. I thought that if this was an example of how efficient the local tradespeople were I would have no worries for the future on this score.

I left Eltisley very early on the morning of Tuesday, 8th November, having loaded the car to the roof with a single divan bed and mattress, two garden chairs, a card table, cooking utensils and other kitchenware such as crockery and cutlery. I took a generous supply of bed clothes, anticipating that nights in the cottage would be quite cold, some towels and other bare essentials as if for a camping expedition.

I had by me two single burner camping gas stoves which had been used on more than one occasion to get us through a power cut and these I loaded knowing that they were now going to come into their own. Along with another one which I had been promised, they would be my lifeline for survival for some time to come. In the derelict kitchen at Overdale there was a switch box for connecting to a cooker which included a plug socket. This would take my electric kettle. Many of the sockets in the house were designed many years before to accept three-pin plugs, the pins being of the round variety. These are now collector's items. There were also some which accepted only two-pin plugs. Fortunately there were a number of such plugs about the house which for the time being might have to be called into service. The kitchen socket was the square-pin type and earthed so that I would feel reasonably safe using it.

I also loaded a proportion of my wardrobe and as I would be likely to be living in the two places, what to take and what to leave was the subject of a series of weighty decisions. I needed above all a full range of working clothes and some to wear on shopping trips and social occasions.

The loading was a hurried affair as I needed to be at Overdale before two o'clock to receive the chimney sweep, otherwise my first set of plans would have disintegrated. I had in mind too that there were some essential items of food I would require for the days ahead. I dealt with this by stopping at Chipping Norton, where I quickly picked up my provisions. Over a period I had found the need to make lists for shopping and for other purposes and because I had this list, my stop was very short.

I arrived in good time to give access to the chimney sweep who was well equipped with large vacuum cleaner and brushes. In no time at all he completed the job which yielded a vast amount of soot. At my request he tipped this in a convenient place in the back garden. I could envisage that after weathering, this would be a most useful commodity to add to the soil, soot being a most valuable source of plant food. When he had finished his task, I paid him and he went cheerfully on his way, no doubt wondering how I was going to exist under such spartan conditions. For my part, I was looking forward with eager anticipation to establishing a base right in the centre where I could get things done.

I had brought with me a three-bar electric convector heater and this I installed in the dining room which for the time being was to become the sitting room and dining room combined, complete with two garden chairs and a card table for furniture. I left most other things in boxes and, having set up my bed in the brightest of the three bedrooms, I began to think of food, for it had been a long day and I was feeling very hungry. The menu for the evening meal was quite ambitious, corned beef and creamed potatoes following by tinned rice pudding. The camping gas stoves behaved impeccably and I produced a simple but satisfactory meal in the knowledge that from now on, the standard could only rise.

In all my visits up to this point I had left the cottage before nightfall but here I was, settling down, hemmed in by the darkness outside but warm, comfortable and replete in the place of my dreams with time stretching before me in which I could indulge in my wildest aspirations. Tomorrow was woodburning stove day and an early start was necessary so a good night's sleep was indicated. Sleep came quickly for the silence of the night at Overdale was remarkable.

Dawn came and I was ready to get started on the day's programme. I had something of a shock when I got out of bed for the house had cooled from the night before and everything I touched seemed cold and clammy, a quick reminder that there really were some acute problems of damp that had to be dealt with. I consoled myself in the knowledge that by the evening, the wood burner would be in place.

I shivered more than somewhat as I took my breakfast in front of the convector heater which had little chance against the cold and damp in the room, but with cereals and a boiled egg inside me, I began to thaw out. A knock at the door heralding the arrival of the stove fitter transformed the situation for there he was complete with The Little Wenlock and ready for action. I was able to help him assemble his requirements and he was soon hard at work. I supplied him with coffee at intervals and this enabled me to tap his knowledge about the stove. By mid-afternoon, the chimney lining had been fitted, the stove put in place and connected to the flue pipe. He tested it briefly by burning some paper to assess the draught control. He declared it to be in a good position and said that it was the ideal stove for the room. He then announced that the fire cement used in installation must dry slowly. This meant leaving it for 24 hours before lighting. This was a major disappointment to me as I wanted to try it out quickly to check whether all my expectations would be fulfilled. He also gave me advice about fuel, to the effect that it would burn almost anything: wood, coal, anthracite, made up fuels, but in his view the best of all was a British Coal product. This was a medium-sized nut which was freely available at most garages and at some shops.

After his departure I drove to the nearest garage in the neighbouring village of Andoversford where to my delight I found a good supply of the recommended fuel in 50 lb bags. I bought two and returned to base and called it a day as far as further work was concerned. I cooked my evening meal over which I read the instruction manual about lighting and managing the wood burner. It had absolutely minimum controls by means of a wheel on the air intake which had a flat round surface. To increase draught it had to be screwed out and vice versa. This appeared to be slightly over-simplified but the manual spoke with consummate confidence about its effectiveness. Tomorrow would prove how true this contention was.

On the following morning because I could not light my precious stove until afternoon I decided to continue with the task of moving the soil away from the outside walls, for this was the first step in dealing with the problem of damp. Until this point, I had convinced myself that the problem could be lived with into the near future but as I had now lived in the house for only two days, the reality was beginning to dawn and something would have to be done. Fortunately the telephone had never been disconnected so I took the bull by the horns. Paul had secured details of several companies who undertook this type of work and I invited three of them to come and make recommendations and supply estimates for the work. They all agreed to visit within the next few days and this surprised me. I learned later that everyone and his grandmother had taken on the role of damp proofing experts.

I continued my outdoor excavations, taking advantage of a spell of fine weather, and started digging at the gable end of the house facing on to the road. It soon became obvious that my idea was correct for I discovered that soil had filled in a gully which carried water away from the foot of the wall. The soil was about two feet deep and its presence was undoubtedly exacerbating the problems of damp in the wall. As mentioned earlier the walls were 24 inches thick and consisted of an outer and an inner layer of Cotswold stone filled in the centre with limestone rubble. Any additional material on the outside was a definite hindrance to a wall drying out.

After lunch, as I could wait no longer, I decided to tackle the ceremonial lighting of The Little Wenlock. I was well prepared with dry kindling and paper firelighters. For the uninitiated, these consist of sheets of *The*

Guardian which are rolled loosely, and then tied into a knot. Care must be taken not to make too tight a knot for air must be able to gain access to the centre of the knotted paper. Access to the stove was through an iron door which takes up most of the front of the stove. The firelighters were laid on the grate and small kindling placed on top. On top again was laid a thin layer of the selected fuel. I closed the draught regulator down to avoid a mad rush of air which might encourage the material to burn too quickly. To my bitter disappointment the whole operation ended in a black pile of paper and sticks which appeared to have no intention of lighting. It seemed that I would have to resort to a system of trial and error and so I prepared another lot of firelighters (my faith in *The Guardian* was beginning to fade) and another pile of sticks. I believed that if I kept the layer of fuel away from the igniting material until it was well ablaze this might work the miracle and sure enough it did. In no time at all the stove became a roaring inferno into which I fed the fuel. Hey presto, success attended my efforts and within an hour there was a warm glow from the stove which soon became too hot to touch. The draught control was everything it claimed to be and in due course I had used all the permutations, from the dull all night burning mode to the open-doored fire, and The Little Wenlock was glowing like a steel furnace and pouring out welcome heat. The man in the shop was right and my stove became the envy of all who visited the house. The room itself was never cold and additionally, heat was spreading to other parts of the house, especially into the bedrooms above. In addition to its qualities as a heat provider, it was aesthetically right for the cottage. It was a dull black and of pre-Victorian design. In other words, it was really very much at home.

The next day, two of the companies bent on carrying out the work of curing the problem of damp turned up as agreed, one in the morning and one after lunch, complete with measuring tapes and clipboards. Both carried with them an instrument designed to measure the levels of humidity. Measurements were taken, damp meter readings recorded and notes made. They were both clearly impressed or horrified depending on where you stood, by the levels of moisture contained in the walls and floors. Beyond rubbing their hands with glee at finding such an ideal case for treatment they gave me a distinct feeling that there was little salvation for my problem other than spending a small fortune on it. They explained all the gruesome details of what would have to be done to cure the problem and promised to send me an estimate as soon as possible. Both representatives exuded an air of competence and confidence but I got a distinct feeling that they were more geared to country manor houses than humble abodes such as mine.

On the Saturday morning the third company arrived, looking as though they might propose starting the job immediately. They were both burly young men but pleasant with it, with accents more commonly found amongst executives rather than artisans. I liked their approach which was not nearly so clinical as their competitors. They gave me the feeling that they really wanted the job. They were positive and realistic, pointing out that there were some essential things to be done and others that could be done but would be of a more cosmetic nature. They also explained what they would actually do and what effect it would have. Basically, this was to drill the walls at floor level and inject a substance which would flood the walls and form a barrier through which rising damp could not penetrate. In the kitchen a different process would be undertaken, called tanking, a highly descriptive word implying that the kitchen on its three damp sides would be like a water tank preventing any seepage into the room. In this case, but not in the other rooms, it would be necessary to chip the plaster off the walls, line the walls and then replaster. This was entirely at odds with the contention of the other two firms.

In all cases injecting with a chemical would be undertaken and in two cases plaster would be chipped off and replaced to a height of three feet, and so I awaited estimates with some trepidation. I had just paid out £44,000 on purchasing the property and new horizons were emerging in terms of renovating costs; it was clear that some limits would have to be placed on these from the start.

With some reluctance I locked up the cottage after lunch on Saturday and headed for Eltisley. I had become very absorbed in the work of renovating and I was enjoying myself. Although in my work of latter years I had spent much time with a pen in my hand, I was happiest when doing things with my hands. Once on the road the whole situation changed for I had one particular event to look forward to and that was a visit to the theatre with Brenda. On Friday I had an appointment with the dentist, glad that I could see her when I was in the area rather than having to make a special trip from Overdale.

Despite all that was happening I had made up my mind that the house at Eltisley should not be neglected. For one thing, if at some stage I was to put it on the market it was important that it should be looking at its best. The same applied to the garden. Doris was a keen and gifted gardener and over

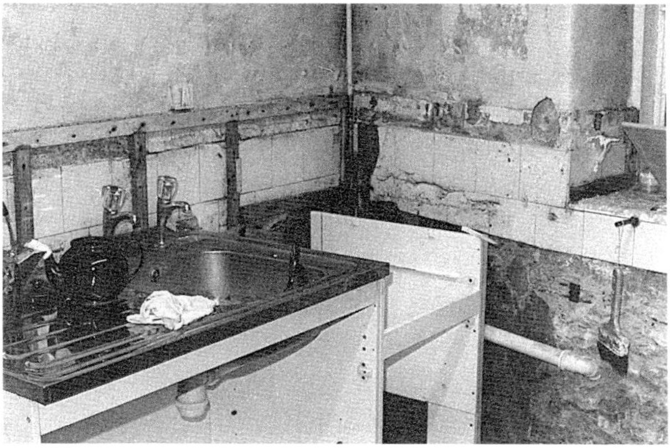

The kitchen

the years had developed a garden which was universally admired. Her knowledge of plants and shrubs was extensive and there was hardly a shrub or plant that she could not identify by its Latin name. She was regarded in the village as an authority on gardens and pot plants (although she would consistently deny this) and her advice was frequently sought by neighbours and friends. It was my determination that the garden should be kept as far as possible to the same standards and since her death I had found that working in the garden through that summer had given me a purpose. The same sentiments applied to keeping our home in similar condition. Working quietly in the house or garden was no burden. It gave me solace to be busy in the place that we had created together and out of which we obtained a good deal of joy and satisfaction.

On arrival I got to work and time passed quickly. My burden was made lighter by the help and support I received from Brenda and occasional shared lunches, but above all a frequent invitation to Sunday lunch. This was always an enjoyable event, starting at 12 o'clock with a liberal supply of sherry, going on into the late afternoon, sometimes extending well into the evening but always with a marked reluctance on my part to return home.

The highlight of the week was a visit to the Cambridge Arts Theatre and although I cannot recall the play, the important thing was that I had the pleasure of the company of such an interesting companion who was an enthusiast for the theatre. Brenda's tastes and mine were similar in many respects, although there were areas in which we did not see eye to eye. I was beginning to persuade myself that our relationship was developing into

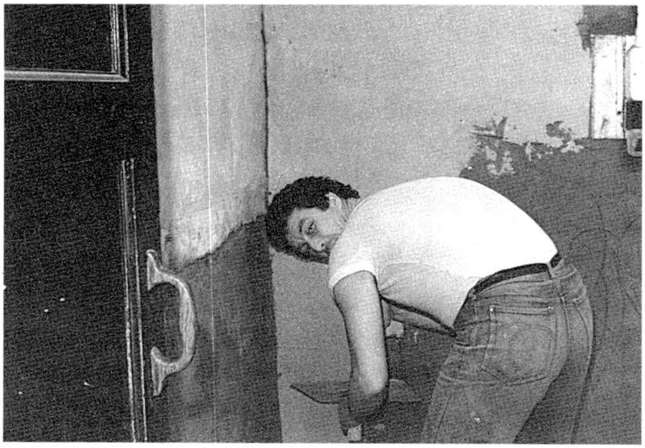

Tanking

more than just friendship but at the same time there were doubts in my mind. As in all such situations there are times when it is difficult to be sure of another person's feelings. I convinced myself that my company was welcomed and this was consolation enough.

Because I needed to act quickly on the matter of damp proofing at Overdale I had asked that the estimates should be sent to my son, thus avoiding any delay in considering them as we were in telephone contact whether I was at Overdale or Eltisley. He telephoned during that week and as I suspected the glossier the presentation, the more expensive the contract was going to be. The glossy brochure, which even contained a photograph of the place where the chemical was manufactured, accompanied by highly technological phraseology running to several pages, advised me that £1,913 would be required to complete the job. The second highest estimate, presented in a less flamboyant manner, was for £1,205. To be fair each of these included chipping off the plaster and renewing it.

I now awaited the third estimate but I was already convinced that they would be given the job. They contended that there was no need to take off the plaster and certainly their logic seemed sound for although the humidity reading was high, the plaster was not soft or crumbling. Plaster on thick Cotswold stone walls is something quite different to the normal situation of plaster over bricks or concrete blocks. When the figures did arrive they were difficult to believe. They undertook to complete the damp proofing of all the downstairs walls and 'tank' the kitchen for the grand total of £360. I telephoned them immediately and asked them to proceed with the job as soon as possible and to let me know the date. I also requested that they should treat the timbers in the roof space against woodworm at the same time. They had looked at this and reported that although there was only slight infestation it would be a wise precaution to treat it. Their estimate was £145 which again was quite competitive. I got early confirmation that they would start the work on 25th November and the timber treatment on a date to be agreed, the reason being that they felt the cottage should not be occupied for at least four days after the treatment.

It seemed to me then and on reflection now, that things were happening at a rapid pace. All very important for the next major steps could not be taken until these were complete. We were in fact into the realms of (to use jargon of those times) critical path analysis which in simple terms meant doing first things first.

My visit to the dentist at the end of the week in Eltisley was uneventful except for the fact that it was the first time I had been treated by a lady, a most pleasant encounter in many ways, not least the skill she demonstrated. One tooth needed filling but this would have to be delayed as I could not fit that in to what was clearly an overcrowded programme. In the meantime she insisted that for my comfort, a temporary filling was essential. This she did, sending me on my way with instructions to return in three weeks' time. This I looked forward to.

On the Tuesday of the next week I returned to Overdale, having heard that Operation Damp Proofing was to commence on the Friday. Although the journey was over a hundred miles it was never tedious, for not only was I driving through some of England's most pleasant countryside, mainly across the Cotswolds, it gave me time to think about plans for the days ahead, and on this particular trip I determined I ought to take time to discuss with Paul and Anne the plans for the holiday cottage project. We needed to share our thoughts on things like charges, changeover of tenants, furnishing and, above all, the sharing of the income it might generate.

One of my main concerns was to ensure that the project should not encroach too much on their very limited time. They were both teachers and, although some might not be aware of it, teaching does not end when school finishes at four o'clock. Much preparation is required for the days ahead, homework and mock exams must be marked and, quite importantly, there is involvement in out of school hours activities such as refereeing team games and supervising teams. Another important task is the development of links with parents.

I also wanted to be sure that the financial arrangements were generous enough to make it worth their while to be involved. My own thoughts were that we should share the profits on a fifty–fifty basis. My input would be the cottage and the cost of equipping it as a holiday cottage, whilst they might handle the administrative work involved in the bookings and supervise the change over of tenants. We would then share the net profit having deducted running costs such as cleaning and administrative expenses. As owner I would meet rates and water rates and any maintenance costs. We agreed to meet formally during that weekend and discuss the details. I drove the twelve pleasant miles through the valley to their house and, after an enjoyable meal, we got down to business.

There was a fair measure of agreement although we debated long and hard on the question of rent levels we ought to charge. I had a certain amount of information with me, gleaned from various sources and I had also had some experience of renting holiday cottages. I tended to use these experiences as a bench-mark, but I believe they felt, although did not want to hurt me by saying so, that the facilities we would be offering would be rather lower than average. They were right up to a point, but in these matters it is not always possible to compare like with like. In addition, we were looking to a time a few months ahead when the cottage would be ready for occupation.

At least our meeting gave us a high level of motivation to get the place ready for occupation as quickly as possible and this would include the purchase of some second-hand furniture. As I was now living in the place, I was able to spend all my time working, apart from sleeping and eating. The daylight hours were short but when the weather permitted I spent time tidying up the immediate vicinity of the house, including the clearing of soil and debris from around the foot of the walls. I also cleaned the paved area at the back of the house which was sheltered by a glazed roof but in a very bad state of repair. The area was like a junk shop, but described in the details as 'conservatory area partly enclosed'. Despite its shortcomings, it afforded a lot of protection to the rear of the house and without it a lot of warmth would have been lost. It was cluttered with old and rotting cupboards and there was a garden in one corner. I cleared everything out of the area including the sunken garden and within days the whole area had changed its character.

A flight of steps gave access to this space from the garden area, the first few yards of which were paved with Cotswold stone. Two doors led from the conservatory, one to the kitchen and the other to the shower and utility room. The ground floor plan on page 26 gives some impression of the house and its surroundings and will assist later as the story of work proceeds.

As promised the two burly men with rather classy accents arrived on the morning of Friday 25th November ready for action on Operation Damp Proofing. Their pick-up truck had seen better days but seemed to bear its heavy load of compressor and chemicals with fortitude. The compressor was unloaded close to the front door and with minimum fuss it was coaxed into action. Compressors react to the demands made on them quite markedly and the noise of the drill, coupled with the oscillating thunder from the compressor, transformed the stillness of the Cotswold morning into tin-pan alley. I looked the other way if anyone came by. I had cleared everything from the outside edges of each room so that work could proceed unhindered and so it did with a minimum of fuss. One could only describe the noise as horrendous and, despite its size, the drill did not penetrate the Cotswold stone with ease. The drilling man worked very hard to make an impact and I could see his relief when his companion took over. I was very thankful that I had no near neighbours for I am sure that life after this would have been something of a problem if there had been anyone living next door.

The first task was to drill holes at six-inch intervals at the foot of all the downstairs walls save the kitchen. Having completed the inside, the process was repeated on the outside walls. With the drilling completed, the next step was relatively easy. The injecting equipment powered by the compressor fed the chemical into the walls, first from the inside and then from the outside. By lunchtime on Saturday, the injection process was complete except for sealing the holes. I was advised that these should be left unsealed in order to allow the chemical to set.

They promised to return on the Monday to start work on the kitchen which was music to my ears. There is a breed of builder which many of us have no doubt met, who start a job today and several weeks later come back to complete it. These two young men were not in that class and although they did have other jobs lined up, their policy was to try and finish one job at a time whenever possible. Their proposal gave me time to prepare well for their return. The task was to clear everything out of the kitchen except the working tops and cupboards on the wall backing on to the dining room. I approached the job with some trepidation for it involved some plumbing skills of which I had none. In the event it turned out to be quite simple for there was a handy stop tap to arrest the flow of water to a cold tap in the sink and a valve which shut off the hot water supply from the hot water storage tank upstairs. These jobs would have been done by the men but our agreement was that I would do these sorts of tasks myself thus minimising costs. Although my plumbing skills were negligible, with the help of a stilsons wrench and an adjustable spanner, I was able to take the taps out of their housing on the sink in preparation for taking out the sink unit. The same applied to the sink wastepipe. This was of the plastic variety and it all virtually came apart in my hands. I could then clear the sink unit and cupboard, and the worktop and cupboard, out into the neighbouring dining room. I then ripped the sheets of hardboard from the walls and in places the plaster came away easily. This was all to the good as most of it had to come off. On completion I stood back and surveyed a most horrible sight and the invasion of damp was very plain to see.

The one sound thing about the kitchen was the floor which was concrete topped with a fine smooth finish and over the whole surface there was no sign of damp. At least one thing was good.

On the Monday true to their word the two young men returned equipped to tackle the stripping off of the plaster. They were clearly pleased to see the preparations I had made and were able to get straight on with the job. In places despite the damp they were obliged to use a mechanical chisel as there was a coating of concrete underneath the plaster which did not yield easily to hand treatment. It was not until well into the second day that the walls were completely bared down to the stone and ready for the new treatment. This process is best described by quoting the statements in the estimate which read as follows, 'hacking off existing plaster and lime to ceiling heights (3 outside walls). Prepare walls for tanking and replastering with a 4:1 sand and cement scratchcoat in Portland cement, sharpwashed sand and waterproof additive. Apply a two coat Thoroseal tanking material to specification, laterally and horizontally to the designated areas.'

The presence of these two young men in the house was a pleasurable experience. They were full of energy and good humour, continually ribbing each other but in a most amicable way without wasting valuable time. The standard of their workmanship was high and when finished, the kitchen was transformed into a bright and cheerful place from what had been a nightmarish hovel.

I had hoped to be able to leave Overdale after about a week and this proved to be possible as the initial cement rendering had to dry out before the final plaster coat could be applied. We agreed that the job would be completed upon my return and I could see rapid progress from now on. With the heating unit installed and the damp proofing complete, other jobs would fit into place, many of which I could do myself without waiting for professional help. The idea of the place being made ready for holiday letting was looking distinctly possible and within the timescale envisaged.

Chapter six

TIME FOR A RE-THINK

Despite my spartan lifestyle at Overdale I was thoroughly enjoying every minute of it. It was a new and vastly different experience and almost every hour of every day presented me with a new challenge, generally of a practical nature but sometimes in the sphere of decision-making. The plan to develop the place as a holiday cottage was uppermost in my mind and this made everything more urgent. There were many jobs to be done to prepare for that time but I also needed to think ahead. For example, there was an urgent need to renew most of the outmoded electrical wiring. How long could I put this off? Ideally there was a need for a bathroom facility upstairs and in due course, central heating ought to be installed.

In the short term, the place could now be prepared as a holiday cottage with little by way of structural work needing to be done. Cleaning and decorating could proceed now that the kitchen was tanked and the walls damp proofed. After that, furnishing would be necessary and by using some of the pieces from Eltisley and purchasing others, it would be made ready for use.

In the early part of December I worked with this in mind, starting by decorating the middle one of the three bedrooms. The other two were in reasonable order. In all cases the paintwork was acceptable subject to a thorough cleaning so my concern was with walls and ceilings only. The whole of the ground floor was white. This was right for the house and so it was only a case of covering white with white and as the ceilings were the same, it was a job which could proceed at a pretty rapid pace.

There were many advantages in living on the job, not least the question of time saving. I could be up early in the morning and after a simple breakfast could be operating often before first light. At the other end of the day I could go on as long as I wished with no need to go through the process of putting away and tidying up. With a plentiful supply of white emulsion the cottage was being gradually transformed.

The cooking facilities were standing up quite well to the demands being made upon them and although the menus lacked a certain amount of variety I fed well and continued to feel very fit on the simple diet. One great consolation I had was access to a daily supply of *The Guardian*. The General Store at Andoversford faithfully kept me a copy each day and so when work was done and my meal consumed, I could do what I have done since I can remember, sit and read this remarkable paper. I confess that in the circumstances of a warm room, a full stomach and genuine tiredness as a result of the hard work of the day, I frequently fell sound asleep, only to wake up often after midnight and then have to drag myself to bed.

In the early part of December I began to harbour some doubts about the idea of Overdale as a holiday cottage. As things stood it would be several months before any income from the cottage would accrue. The overheads on two houses were significant and there was something of a problem about furniture. As I would continue to live at Eltisley, some furniture would be retained there, and the rest moved to Overdale. In due course, if and when I decided to move to Overdale and cease to let it, a further movement of furniture would have to be undertaken. This all seemed quite costly. Letting it for holidays would frustrate my original purpose of spending my time undertaking the renovations. It seemed that I was fast losing sight of my original objective of finding a challenge.

I had earlier registered my intention of leaving Eltisley by seeking a valuation on my house and undertaking to give my agents the option of selling it when the time arrived. It was a period of uncertainty which had given rise to other questions. If I did intend to sell, it would have to be with vacant possession and this implied removing my furniture from the house ahead of the agreed possession date. I also knew that it was not easy to secure the services of a removal company at the drop of a hat. They would require several weeks' notice of the date.

Uppermost in my mind and colouring all my thoughts was my friendship with Brenda. I was always happy in her company and I took every opportunity of visiting her on the slightest excuse. I knew deep down however that these feelings were not reciprocated. My vanity led me to believe that she found my company enjoyable and we had shared lots of good times together but I also felt that our relationship had not progressed beyond this point. She was generous and kind to me and when I felt troubled she had the capacity to help me through the state of depression. It was a time of peaks and troughs emotionally and she contributed much to keeping me from the depths of despair. It was becoming apparent that sooner or later I would have to come to terms with the fact that my wishes for a future development of our relationship would have to be abandoned but whilst there was any shred of hope I would continue to seek out her company.

On my next visit to Eltisley I decided to explore the idea of removing my furniture to Overdale, first the likely cost and then the question of length of notice required. There was no problem in securing interest in my request for an estimate as the first three names I telephoned promised to visit within the next few days. I had taken the precaution of measuring doorways, entrances and stairways at Overdale for owing to its age and shape, there was nothing standard. Several doorways were narrower than average and the stairway was quite restricted. I also drew a plan of the house. This was quite a useful preparation for the removal people. Anything which was on the large side was measured and fortunately they were all convinced that there would be no insuperable problems in the move. They all stated that they would require two to three weeks' notice of the date of removal for the distance involved meant that two full days would be required for the operation.

In due course I received three quotations and, as is often the case, there was a huge difference between them all. The highest was double the price of the lowest. One is often forced to the conclusion that some quotations are based on the premise that the sender does not want the job at any price and to ensure that they do not get it, they send an impossible estimate. I accepted the lowest estimate in writing stating that it might be some time before I would know the date of my removal.

During that week I kept my appointment with my dentist and again thoroughly enjoyed the treatment which consisted of a filling. I now felt that I could forget my teeth for some time to come. I had some slight misgivings about this as my two visits had been so pleasurable that I could have happily continued to subject myself to the lady's attentions on a regular basis. I found it hard to think of a reason why I should seek another appointment however.

The following day was another most pleasant one as I had been invited to a meal with Pam, I arrived, at about 6.30 pm. There was much to talk about and much upon which I needed advice. As I have emphasised, Pam was a good listener and I wanted to put her in the picture about what I had been doing since we last met. As I reflected again on these meetings, I believe I must have done most of the talking and possibly to the point of boredom for Pam. If it were so, she never gave me the impression that this was the case and her support and advice was most valuable to me. I always came away feeling much elated, for on each occasion her hospitality was unbounded and her cooking excellent. I tended to stay late into the night and with about an hour's drive home, I was getting into bed long after midnight. On this occasion I left knowing that we would meet again on 23rd December as she had invited me to a party she was giving. This date went into my diary and although it was very full, I was determined not to miss this forthcoming event.

A few days later I set off for Overdale where I intended to be for as long as possible until the Christmas break. On each of my journeys I carried things for which I had a need and, if possible, things which I would not need to take back. As I was now likely to be needing carpentry and building tools I made a selection of these and I also packed my range of decorating tools including a substantial stepladder. The addition of my Black and Decker workbench now left me with limited space which I had reserved for several tins of white emulsion paint, plaster mix, Polyfilla, putty and sundry other items.

My intention was to call at Bedford on my journey and find the material at lowest cost by some shopping around. I was religiously pursuing a policy of keeping costs to the minimum possible and, however small the item, I would seek it out on this basis. Although the process took more time, this was of no consequence for the money was limited whereas my time was not. Apart from everything else, shopping became a positive and interesting exercise in itself. I also tried to pursue this policy in my food shopping and had found a small supermarket in Chipping Norton where I could buy at cheaper prices than most other places and where I could park on the doorstep with minimum fuss. I fulfilled both of my intentions on my journey, arriving at Overdale as darkness was falling. I lit the fire before unloading the car and by the time I had carried the tools and equipment indoors, the house was beginning to warm up and it was time to cook my evening meal.

I had a most pleasant surprise when I went outside the following morning for I had almost forgotten that I had negotiated for a job to be done and during my absence, it had been carried out. This was one of many jobs which I had found needed doing from a closer examination of the building after I had taken it over. The gutterings all round the house were of cast iron and in places were rusted and broken as were some of the downpipes.

The whole of it needed to be renewed for safety reasons and also because there were several places where, when it rained, the water from the roof was finding its way into the walls and also falling at the foot of the walls. The person concerned had been recommended to me and after an examination of the job, he had submitted an estimate which I accepted. The job was listed to be done at an unspecified date. As I climbed the steps into the garden my eyes fell on a pile of old guttering stacked in a neat pile on the ground and on turning round, saw to my delight that it had all been replaced by black polythene pipes and guttering. This was going to be a big practical improvement and at the same time, it vastly enhanced the look of the property. The complete job cost £175 and was another valuable and economical improvement, executed without delay or fuss. I began to ask myself if this was all down to beginner's luck. Could it all go as smoothly as this or would I sooner or later come up against a really big problem? I saw no reason to think so and as I am also an incurable optimist, I persuaded myself that all would be well.

I now settled down to several days of indoor decorating and with little relief, other than a brief stop for lunch. The daylight hours were at their shortest and so I had to rely on artificial light for a fair proportion of the time and this made the job more difficult, particularly when ceilings were being done. There is a theory that when the days are short and the weather wintry, the human spirit falls to a low ebb and this might have accounted for the fact that after several days with brush in hand, my spirits began to sag. What had up to now been an exciting and exhilarating adventure suddenly became a heavy burden and the rhythm of work fell dramatically. Late one afternoon, I suddenly felt desperately alone, a feeling which I thought I had conquered. Here I was in the middle of nowhere, forcing myself to keep going at a task which for the time being I had no heart for and in which, at that particular time, I could see little point. For a time I felt I had reached rock bottom and I needed to talk to someone. The nearest and the ones who I knew had the capacity to help were Cynthia and Roy in Cheltenham only a few miles away. I took the bull by the horns and telephoned them. Roy answered the phone and it was a relief to hear his calm and reassuring voice. His immediate reaction was that I should get in my car and drive down to see them. He instantly suspected that all was not well.

When I arrived he was preparing to go to work as he was on night duty but the short conversation we had brought me back to some degree of stability and I spent the rest of the evening unburdening myself to Cynthia. In this welcoming and secure atmosphere with a drink and some food inside me, I began to throw off the despondency that had overtaken me. By midnight I had recovered my composure and I took my leave and returned to Overdale admonishing myself slightly for not being able to deal with the situation unaided. I feel sure that many people who suffer a breakdown could often avoid it if they could find the right person to share their burden with at the time. This was one of the many attributes which Cynthia possesses in good measure. Despite the many tragic situations she had experienced she has a sense of fun which is quite infectious. At the same time she has an instinctive understanding of other people's problems which she is willing to share. The following morning I awoke ready to tackle the day and in a much improved state of mind.

On Saturday Paul and Anne came over bringing amongst other things a plentiful supply of food for the day, buckets, brushes and some garden tools. I believe they might have sensed from telephone conversations that I was somewhat overwhelmed by the tasks ahead. Their plan was to make a start on tidying up the garden and certainly there was a great need for this if some order was to be restored by the spring. Although the winter weather had made its own contribution, much could be done to find the borders from the mass of weeds and this they did to good effect. At the end of the day one could see where the lawn stopped and the borders began and in the borders, shrubs and perennial plants started to appear through the undergrowth. They worked outside until the light began to fade and then came indoors to give an hour or two of their decorating skills.

It was good having them about the place and I believe they enjoyed the challenge. At the same time I think they wondered whether it was going to be possible to make the idea of the holiday cottage a reality. I am sure they wondered too whether I had made the right decision by buying the cottage in the first place in view of all the work which needed to be done. Despite the doubts I sensed in their minds, they were unstinting in their practical help and support and at the end of that weekend, the cottage was taking on the look of a place that someone cared about.

Christmas was fast approaching and I had been given an invitation to spend it with Paul and Anne, coupled with advice that I ought to take a short break from work at Overdale. I looked forward with great pleasure to a relaxing time with them and I knew their hospitality would be unbounded. In the four days before returning to Eltisley I devoted time to carrying the renovation of the kitchen a stage further. This consisted of putting the sink unit back in place together with the cupboard and the worktop. I had delayed doing this to allow a period for the walls to dry out. Another reason was that it was a two-man job. As luck would have it I had word from my brother-in-law, Harry, from Cheltenham, telling me that he would be visiting. I had carried out some minor repairs to the unit as it stood free in the dining room and with Harry's help we put the unit in place. By great good fortune it went back perfectly. The trick was to ensure that the taps, the unit and the pipes would all line up. We were working within severe limits of 3 mm but no one was more surprised than I when the whole thing lined up within these limits and as a consequence, the reconnection of hot and cold water taps to the pipes was simple as was the reconnection of the waste pipes. To complete the job I hung the doors of the unit and the cupboard and set the worktop in place, locating the securing screw holes with minimum trouble. At the end of the day I had restored the kitchen furniture to its rightful place and just as important, had cleared the dining room of the obstacles which I had been negotiating for several weeks at great inconvenience. It was not a room which could have been shut off as I had to go through it to the front door, the sitting room and the staircase leading to the first floor.

I had now arrived at a point where I could say that the real priority jobs had been completed and I could see some order developing out of the chaos. The house was beginning to dry out and felt warmer when I entered it now, in stark contrast to the days before the woodburner was installed and damp proofing completed. With walls which were 24 inches thick there was no doubt that once heat had been generated inside, it took some time for the house to cool. The insulation of these walls is quite something and of course, in a hot summer, the reverse is true for these houses are remarkably cool in the heat, when we are lucky enough to get such weather.

So now everything could wait until after the Christmas break. I turned off the water, left things reasonably tidy and set off on the road back to Eltisley. It would have been far more sensible to have gone straight to Milton-under-Wychwood, but I had important engagements in Cambridge, one long-standing invitation and others which I hoped might materialise. When I got home I found an excuse to go and see Brenda and I had no hesitation in accepting her invitation to have lunch with them on Christmas Eve. I felt extremely lucky because in addition to the new invitation, I was to attend a party to be given by Pam on the evening of 23rd December. Together with my planned stay with Paul and Anne over

Christmas, my holiday was complete. My need for the company of friends had not diminished and I was grateful.

Pam's party was particularly enjoyable in that I met several friends whom I had not seen since my retirement and there was a lot of reminiscing about our days at work together, particularly the funny experiences we shared. As is usual on these occasions, much of the talk centred around people and their idiosyncrasies including our own. It was certainly not malicious gossip but the real stuff of which good parties are made. They were all particularly interested in my accounts of domestic life on my own and somewhat amazed at my knowledge of the finer points of washing, cleaning and cooking. Just as men find it hard to believe that a woman is capable of many of the so called 'men's jobs', women see men as totally undomesticated. Their view of me was one built on the work situation and they found it difficult to imagine me standing at an ironing board.

Our hostess Pam had provided abundantly and the table rocked under the weight of some excellent food but for some unaccountable reason, the beer ran out. One would have thought she had made ample provision of beer but an unusually large number of people turned down whisky, gin and other exotic beverages in favour of beer. By great good fortune someone knew a man who would have a supply of beer and I volunteered to go with him to collect it in my car, unknown to the guests. Pam took it all in her stride and kept a cool head, making as usual the perfect hostess. We all agreed with one accord that it had been a wonderful party and a good start to Christmas. We took our leave and went our separate ways home. It was by now Christmas Eve.

After a short night I was up early for I had a full schedule, some cleaning, one or two courtesy calls to make in the village and above all, loading my car for a return to the Cotswolds and to Paul's. As usual I loaded things needed for the next phase of work at Overdale. This time I concentrated on some garden tools, stepladder, workbench and a wide range of building and carpentry tools for as far as I could see, I would not need any of these things again at Eltisley.

My lunch appointment with Brenda was getting closer quite rapidly but as usual I was attempting to do more than was possible in the time. I wanted to have everything ready for departure to the Cotswolds before I went and it was something of a scramble. Life was very crowded and I liked it that way. None of it was of particular importance to anyone except me and it had become a way of life. It was at least constructive and at the same time, instructive, allowing me to experiment without doing anyone any harm. As to whether it was a benefit to anyone else it is difficult to say. I gained considerable satisfaction from what I was doing and that seemed very important.

Brenda provided an excellent lunch and we were all in very good spirits. As a qualified nursing sister Brenda had a quite exacting job at the local hospital but because she had a young family, she was not called upon for duty over the Christmas period. She was totally relaxed and in her most witty frame of mind so that lunch took on the atmosphere of a party, the second in two days for me. After lunch we sat in front of a real log fire and conversation flowed freely and I was enjoying it all. The time passed quickly and I started to be a little concerned about my promise to be with Paul and Anne reasonably early on Christmas Eve, when we would have a meal together. Despite my reference to this, I was pressed into staying a little longer and it was finally suggested that it was a pity to break up the party and that I should delay my journey to the Cotswolds until the next day. I am bound to say that the temptation to stay longer was in conflict with my promise to Paul and Anne. In the end my commitment to Paul and Anne prevailed and I had to say that I would go.

As I took my leave and drove into the night, I pondered on the events of the day. Certainly it had been most enjoyable and I had been given a warm and generous welcome but did the slight pressure on me to stay longer stem from the momentary enchantment of the event, or was it a concern for my safety on such a journey at the end of a long day? With hindsight now, I believe I read too much into what happened although at the time it gave me quite a boost. When you get the feeling that your company is valuable, it does something for your ego. I travelled *lightly* on that Christmas Eve.

I arrived at Paul and Anne's full of apologies which they accepted unreservedly. I think now that my behaviour was most reprehensible for after all, their invitation to stay was of long standing and I had seen fit not to be there at the time which we had agreed. I could offer no excuses other than that time had passed by without my realising it, a feeble excuse without a doubt. My offence was not held against me and we had a most enjoyable Christmas for in addition to the most wonderful seasonal fare, we undertook two small tours of the Cotswolds interspersed with spells of walking in the crisp winter countryside. I remember vividly a short stay in Stow-on-the-Wold where we enjoyed a snack lunch in the Falcon Hotel which had been tastefully decorated for Christmas.

We did not spend much time discussing the holiday cottage project but I believe I was probably giving signs, subconsciously, of having some doubts about it. This must have been somewhat annoying to them although they did not show it. I can only say in defence that I was in a period of uncertainty. My friendship with Brenda and with other people at Eltisley left me with a feeling of wanting to be in both places at one and the same time, but after some reflection I decided to allow the Eltisley house to go on the market. It might not sell all that quickly by which time my personal affairs might have sorted themselves out. In any case I was somewhat concerned about the short-term implications of maintaining two houses, one of which was the subject of a quite substantial loan.

I spent several days at Overdale after Christmas and although doubts were beginning to arise about the holiday cottage project, there seemed to be no need to make any changes in the plans for restoring the place. One thing which would change, however, was that if the Eltisley property sold quickly and possession was required immediately, then within a short time I would be removing my furniture to Overdale to comply with the undertaking given in the contract. With this in mind, the key areas to consider were the floors in all rooms for it would be unfortunate if furniture had to be moved from one room to another to allow me to do what was required. I therefore embarked on a plan for cleaning and checking all the floors. All the bedroom floors were in reasonable condition but needed cleaning and scrubbing. By this time I had transferred one of my two vacuum cleaners to Overdale so that the first stage was easy and that was followed by a thorough scrubbing of the boards. At this time, as I did frequently during the whole operation, I thought about what life must have been like before the invention of the vacuum cleaner. It and the wheel must be amongst the world's greatest inventions. I rolled back the carpets half way in each room to scrub the boards and then reversed the process.

On the ground floor the sitting room was of particular interest with its original flagstone floor. My intention in the long term was to leave it bare with perhaps a mat in the fireplace area. At this stage I cleaned and washed it, putting the carpet back until such time as I could work at it in an attempt to restore it to its original condition. The dining room required special attention as there were traces of damp in several places arising from the fact that the concrete floor had been laid without a concrete membrane. The only solution was to treat it with a sealer compound of which two coats were recommended. As the second coat could not be applied until two days after the first, this was the last job I did before returning to Eltisley. It turned out to be an interesting exercise in logistics in view of the fact that the material remained tacky for about 12 hours after application and that the whole surface had to be completed in one operation. As this room was a thoroughfare, once the application had been made it became out of bounds for foot traffic. I had to make sure that all I required to take with me from upstairs was ready to hand on the ground floor but I also had to ensure that I could somehow cross the floor in the morning from the bottom of the stairs to the kitchen and thereby make my escape. This was accomplished by means of a bridge consisting of a long plank from the stairs to the kitchen doorway. The system worked perfectly and I also knew that I could use the system on the second application which I intended to do as the first job on my return.

As I travelled home my thoughts were focused on the need to make a decision about the Eltisley house. The agents had now gone ahead with the advertising and it was likely that a prospective purchaser would come forward. If this happened I had to make a decision which could not be hedged about with conditions of uncertainty. I came to the conclusion that if a prospective buyer came along I had no option but to agree to sell. For the moment I did not want to think beyond that point. Let the future take care of itself.

Chapter seven

NO TURNING BACK

I arrived at Eltisley feeling that this was likely to be a period during which I would need to face up to reality and sure enough, within a couple of days things began to happen. I had a telephone call from the agents to say they had found a prospective buyer who would like to see the house with a view to purchase. They had sold their own house and could proceed. We agreed a date and time and within a few hours of this happening, I had a call from a neighbour who said that her son and daughter-in-law would like to buy the house, could they come and see it? I had to tell her that I would be glad to show them over the house but that I had another party who were wanting to buy subject to an inspection which had been arranged. I made the point that I was duty bound to allow this to proceed but that should the people not want to purchase, I would immediately contact her.

The prospective buyers, man, wife and child, arrived and it was clear from the start that they liked the house and in particular the lady, who was much attracted by the garden. It was a somewhat difficult encounter for the little girl was of the hyperactive type who could not keep still and wanted to pick up everything in sight. Dad had to carry her around the house to which she strongly objected. Despite the distraction, we were able to have a full discussion which ended in a firm offer to pay the asking price. This I gladly accepted. When a sale is accomplished as quickly as this and without complications, one is left with a feeling that the price was fixed too low. This did not concern me too much for it was pleasing to know that someone had found the place attractive enough to buy it without hesitation. We agreed that possession would be given on completion of the contract which I assured the buyer would be just as quickly as he wished for I knew my solicitor would deal expeditiously with the exchange. We were thinking of an early February date. Their serious intention to buy was signalled by a request that I should allow them to bring certain plants and shrubs from their own garden and heel them into mine.

The die was now cast and I began to plan my move to take place in early February. I contacted the removal company to agree a date and other details, such as that they would pack all china and glass and I would do the rest. The date was to be 3rd February and they would load the day before, ready to move off early next morning. I was now able to make plans for the big day and to determine whether I could do anything to facilitate a smooth operation. I had undertaken to leave behind all the floor coverings and curtains on the ground floor as these had been professionally laid and hung and would not have fitted easily into any other premises. I did have a use for the carpets upstairs and decided to move these to Overdale in my car and if possible to lay them before the day of removal. As there were several weeks before the move I felt I should limit my tasks to the upper floor, leaving the ground floor as undisturbed as possible until nearer the moving date. This still left me with plenty of preparation work for I could start packing the tools from my workshop, the garden tools, books and kitchen utensils. All of these threw up a need for stout cardboard boxes and my only solution was to garner an extra box or two on each occasion on which I did my food shopping. One could find a fine selection at any supermarket checkout area and soon I had assembled what I thought was an adequate collection. These I gradually packed on my visits during the next few weeks.

I informed Brenda of my imminent departure, which appeared not to come as any surprise to her, and at the same time I said that I had a number of appointments I would need to come back for, over the months ahead. She generously invited me to stay on these occasions. This was my lifeline as I could not contemplate cutting myself off from so many friends in East Anglia and in particular ending my contact with Brenda. I now felt content that I had the best of both worlds, the continuing and absorbing interest of living and working at Overdale interspersed with regular visits to Eltisley. The prospects ahead were indeed pleasant.

One small cloud on the horizon worried me a lot and that was my promise to Paul and Anne about the joint enterprise of the holiday cottage. I had a strong sense that I was letting them down, particularly because they had spent time and effort in helping to prepare Overdale for the project. In the event I raised the matter with some trepidation but they did not appear to be too disappointed about the change of plan. I could only hope that I had not let them down too badly. They had given me a lot of support and were not critical in any way of my actions now.

Having done as much as I could for the time being at Eltisley I returned to Overdale complete with carpets, etc., with the aim of making ready for the arrival of the furniture. I had completed the sealing of the dining room floor and could now lay the carpet from Eltisley which was almost tailor-made for the space, with a minimum of cutting. The change brought about by this single act was quite dramatic for the carpet was of a particularly high quality, almost plain and the colour of clover. It replaced a rather drab gold carpet of unsuitable quality for a Cotswold cottage. Against the pristine white of the walls it brought a richness to the room which I knew would be absolutely right to house my dark oak furniture. The carpet in the sitting room was quite beyond redemption and this I replaced with the plain dark grey from Eltisley; again the ideal colour and quality for this stone flagged floor. I was quite delighted that purely by chance I appeared to have the ideal solution to the floor covering problem. All this gave me renewed enthusiasm to return to my decorating of which there was still plenty to keep me occupied.

I now began to consider what needed to be done amongst the major items of work which I had listed earlier in my long-term plan of renovation. Although for my own private needs the shower room on the ground floor, which included a wash basin and a toilet, was adequate, it would not be acceptable to guests. It was far too spartan an arrangement apart from the fact that it was a day's journey to reach it from the bedrooms, necessitating the opening of four doors. Overdale needed something in keeping with the 1980s. I had two options: one was to update the existing shower room and install a bath thus making the whole thing warmer and more comfortable, or alternatively to convert the end bedroom into a bathroom. The latter plan would ensure the development of a luxury facility as the room was 14 feet by 7 feet 6 inches and could be suitably furnished. The disadvantage of course was the loss of a bedroom, an important factor to consider. On the ground floor the room which had been a workshop could be adapted as a study/bedroom as it was adjacent to the shower room. I therefore decided that the main bathroom should be on the first floor near to the bedrooms. With limited knowledge of costs I had some doubts about the practicality of converting this bedroom. It was at the furthest point from the sewerage system and I could envisage the possibility of high costs if trenching and pipe laying had to be undertaken. As a first step I decided to visit the suppliers of bathroom equipment in Cheltenham in order to obtain some basic costs. This proved to be an interesting and enjoyable expedition for the choice was wide and varied and prices seemed to me to be remarkably reasonable. I did not think I needed the luxury of gold plated taps nor yet a round sunken bath but amongst the conventional suites there was a good selection. I opted for an ivory coloured suite at a modest total cost of £189 plus VAT, asking them to withhold delivery until such time as I could accommodate it. I was of the opinion if the equipment could be obtained so cheaply I could afford the costs involved in the installation.

In the nearby village of Northleach there was an ironmonger's shop which also had a plumbing and central heating department. The latter was run by the son who, within a few days of my request, came to view the job prior to submitting an estimate. I was most pleasantly surprised to learn from him that there were no practical problems arising from the location of the proposed bathroom. With modern materials the outflow pipes could be carried to any distance and to any point. It turned out to be a fairly short run to the nearest sewage pipe and the water pipes again had a relatively short distance to run to the connection point. This was all good news but the final piece of information was the most welcome of all when the young man announced that, as this was a necessary improvement, the whole job would be zero rated for VAT. My hopes rose as it began to appear that the whole project could be accomplished at reasonable cost and I was delighted to read that installing the whole system would cost £584. Adding this to the payment of £225 for the suite meant that I would have a new luxury bathroom for £800. A certain amount of tiling would have to be done but as this was something I could do myself, the cost of the tiles would be the end of my expenditure on this project.

As the installation of the bathroom was likely to be one of the largest items of expenditure I was confident that I could proceed with other major works and keep within my budgets. Needless to say, I telephoned the company in Northleach and asked them to start the work as soon as possible.

As 2nd February was fast approaching, I now had to stop all work at Overdale other than preparing to receive the furniture, and having done this I set off for Eltisley with an additional supply of boxes for packing purposes. As I started to pack I could not escape the feeling of some distress and sadness. The house was full of memories of life with Doris and our daughter Anne, over a period of sixteen years. Although Anne had only lived in the house for three years, memories of her still being there were very strong. There was a sense in which I felt I was deserting them by leaving, but in a more rational frame of mind, I realised that they would not have wanted me to otherwise. I had to pull myself together and get on with my plans for there was plenty to do in the three days I had allowed before 2nd February arrived.

Although it is strictly illegal there were certain shrubs and plants I was determined to take from the garden. They were special items which Doris had propagated from cuttings given to her by friends. They had flourished under her care and whatever else was left behind, these would go, and I carefully lifted and root-wrapped them ready for the journey. I also packed a collection of pot plants which had graced the house for many years.

I had been advised not to pack any clothes from wardrobes for new techniques for house removals had been developed and the mobile wardrobe hanging frames were indeed a labour saver. Cardboard boxes abounded everywhere containing books, pots, pans, kitchenware and in the garage another selection held tools, paint, nails, screws and all the accumulation of a life of do-it-yourself activity. The final act of taking down the curtains was done in the morning of the arrival of the removal van.

By lunch time the van was loaded and after taking leave of my neighbours I departed for Overdale, and as I crossed the green and out on to the main road, the feelings of regret overtook me again, although I knew for certain now that there was no turning back. The decision had been made and I would have to learn to live with it. Even reflecting on the euphoric feeling I had experienced when I made up my mind to buy Overdale I could not dispel the deep feelings of regret which had settled in my mind as I travelled westward.

The next 48 hours were a nightmare full of self pity and remorse which I could not shake off. It was like wandering between two worlds, one of which was finished and the other not yet come to life. I had no appetite for food or drink and I slept only fitfully, getting out of bed early with a desperate feeling of loneliness upon me and in no state to meet the challenge of what was going to be an extremely busy and heavy day.

I had worked on a plan of action for dealing with the furniture when it arrived but I could not give my mind to it. The removal van arrived much earlier than I had expected and this coupled with my own loss of motivation and energy led to a most chaotic day. Because I could not concentrate, many of the things ended up in the wrong place. I took the easy way out and if uncertain I asked them to put things wherever they could find space. Fortunately the largest pieces of furniture did end up in the right places but many of the boxes and other items were dropped wherever there was room.

The two men were very helpful but also anxious to get on their way back to Huntingdon, more particularly I think because there was a threat of snow. They did not relish crossing the Cotswolds in a snowstorm which I know can sometimes be quite hair-raising.

I was not sorry when the last items came off and they departed because I felt I needed some time on my own and above all, I needed a rest. As the lorry pulled away from the cottage there was a knock on the door; this was the last thing I needed. I answered it to find the local vicar smiling warmly. He had just called to welcome me to the village. I tried to contain my feelings but I suspect he must have regarded me as a rather dubious newcomer. I acknowledged his kind gesture for I knew his intentions were of the best, and at a later date when we met again I apologised for what must have seemed my very strange behaviour. When he departed I sat amongst the ruins contemplating my next move. Overdale had taken on the appearance of a badly organised antique shop and movement around was severely restricted.

After a while I started to come to life as I suddenly realised that I had to pull myself together and make a start on bringing some order out of the chaos. I worked first on clearing a pathway to the kitchen and making a space in the dining room where I might sit to eat and gradually my pace of work increased in momentum. It seemed that the most sensible plan was first to make sure that I could get access to my bedroom then to other parts of the house without moving anything too far at this stage. The next time anything was moved it should go into its permanent position as far as possible. As I worked on, I reflected on why I of all people should have ended up in this unholy mess. Had I not spent a lot of time in the last few years at work running courses on work and method study? Here was a good example of the phrase 'If you can't do it, teach'. I hoped that the last hour or two had only been a temporary aberration.

As I had made an early start to the day there came a point when I felt I had had enough and this was the signal for making a simple meal. Before preparing this I determined that I would fix up my music centre and locate the tapes and records which I had carefully packed. Within half an hour the house was filled with music and as I was wanting to be cheered up, I made a choice from my collection of Gilbert and Sullivan records, good music coupled with clever lyrics and, after all these years, still speaking eloquently to the times we live in, urging those in authority not to take themselves too seriously. The music, the food and the biting sarcasm of the lyrics was just what I needed and in due course I retired to bed in a quiet and satisfied state of mind, sleeping soundly until dawn.

My preoccupation the following morning after breakfast was to get the cooker operational. There was a connecting box on the wall and although I usually avoided doing anything except the most simple tasks with electrical circuits, I felt that it would not be too difficult to connect the cooker to the box. I took off the front only to find that it was not as simple as I thought. I often think that these things are made so that an amateur cannot deal with them and there may be some logic in this. One mistake with electricity can be lethal. After a struggle I thought I had just about solved it although I had some lingering doubts. I decided to try it out and replaced the cover on the box believing that if I had not got it right the worst that could happen would be a blown fuse. I switched on and nothing happened. Keeping my fingers crossed I then switched on the hotplate which to my surprise started to warm up. I was just congratulating myself when I heard the noise of the trip switch going. I waited a few minutes and restored the trip switch only to find it slipping straight out again. Discretion seemed to be the better part of valour in these circumstances. There were many well-recorded incidents of people being electrocuted as a result of trying to do things with electricity when their knowledge was limited. I was well aware of the dangers and yet stupid enough to try it out. Fortunately the telephone directories were still in the house, left by the previous owners, and I made a short list of electricians who were offering their services. The first one I rang was out on a job but his wife promised to get him to ring me when he came in which he did shortly afterwards. Although he was in Cheltenham some seven miles away, he said he would come after lunch. I could not believe my good fortune in getting help so quickly.

On his arrival he expressed some horror at the fact that I had tried to do the job myself but seeing the state of upheaval in the house and observing my plight, he clearly had some sympathy and soon connected the cooker according to the regulations. When he came to test it the hotplate refused to get hot and he diagnosed that it had been burned out in the process of my switching on the cooker which had been incorrectly connected. All the other elements were working but as this was the only hotplate it was clear that the element must be renewed. What surprised me was his offer to return to Cheltenham and obtain a new element and within the hour he was back, fixed the element and tested the complete job. I was eternally grateful for all this and made the point to him also offering to pay his account. This he declined saying he would submit it in due course. When it came it was most reasonable and I happily paid it immediately. It seemed to me that once again the business people in this area did their very best to please the customer. In his case it was particularly interesting as he obviously had plenty of work in hand and had interrupted this to get me out of trouble. On parting he said that he felt I ought to have the whole place rewired and that I should get someone to look at it. This was not a plea for a job as he had already stated that he had more work than he needed.

With the cooker now working and the refrigerator plugged in and in place, I could bring some order into my culinary affairs and pack away the three camping gas stoves which had served me so well. There were also many items in boxes which would take their place in the kitchen in due course and as I came across them in all corners of the cottage, I deposited them in their proper place.

I spent the next few days bringing order out of chaos. This involved placing all the main items of furniture in their chosen places and as the heaviest of these had been put where they should be on delivery, it was relatively easy. What pleased me most of all was the fact that all the items were absolutely right for the house being mostly made of oak. There was also more space in some rooms than at Eltisley and as a consequence they showed themselves off better.

The bedroom I had been using had looked very much like a slum, for all the bits and pieces were very much a makeshift. I decided that it was time I slept in a more dignified environment and so I concentrated next on setting this to rights. Again as the furniture had been carried to the room by the removers it was a simple enough task once I had decided where everything should go. After making a decision as to where the bed should go and taking into account the positions of the door and windows, all other items fell naturally into place. This was a most pleasant master bedroom some 15 feet by 14 feet, one window looking out on to the village green and the other, at the front, on to the valley below and across the gently undulating slopes above which were divided by lines of rich Cotswold stone walls, and often populated by sheep.

As my days as a commuter were now at an end, I was beginning to feel that the time had come when I ought to acknowledge at least to myself that I was now a member of the community of Shipton Oliffe. I had of course seen my nearest neighbours as they passed along in front of Overdale on their way to the village but had not yet had the opportunity of doing more than passing the time of day with them. I needed to correct this omission at the earliest opportunity. Their house, known as College Farm, which I could see from the window in the southern gable end of Overdale, was a typical Cotswold stone farmhouse of high quality with a series of outbuildings in the same style. I later learned that their names were Austin and Lorelei and in due course found them to be of a most friendly and helpful disposition. From the start they took an almost fatherly and motherly interest in my welfare and showed me great kindness. Austin farmed about 80 acres of mostly pasture on which he kept a most unusual flock of black sheep. These were his pride and joy but his abiding interest was his hunter which he used to get around his land, in addition to hunting. He was very much at home on his horse and was clearly an excellent horseman. There was obviously a great bond between horse and man, conveyed by their every movement, and on the move they were as one.

Austin and Lorelei had great affection for the village and its people, not in a patronising way but genuinely from a caring point of view. Austin's bluff straightforward manner masked a concern for others and many good deeds of which many were unaware. A conversation with him acted as a tonic for he had a great love of life and had a wide and interesting experience of many aspects of it. A well-remembered act of kindness came quite early on. At the top of the steps at the back of the house, the previous owners had deposited an old and very heavy iron bath which had been taken out of the shower room, presumably when the shower was installed. This was an eyesore and a particular irritant as one looked out of the back windows. It had also acted as a depository for old pipes and cast iron guttering. I was preparing to depart for Eltisley one Friday morning when Austin was passing by on horseback. He stopped his horse at the back gate and in the middle of our conversation he pointed to the old bath, saying that if I had no use for it he would have it carted away. I had no plans to use it and expressed my gratitude for his kind offer. Imagine my delight when I returned to Overdale to find the bath and its contents gone. I was profuse in my thanks but it was clear that he did not regard his act as anything more than a neighbourly gesture. To me it was an enormous help for the bath was so heavy that I had no transport capable of carrying it. There were many more such acts of kindness to follow including an offer to keep an eye on the cottage when I was away. He said it would be useful for him to have a key in case anything drastic should happen. Having handed him a key I then felt completely at ease about leaving the place at any time. In the light of all his help and kindness I looked for opportunities to repay him in some way or other but on one occasion when I mentioned this, his view was that they were pleased that I had come along and was bringing the cottage and its garden back to life after a long period of near dereliction. This made me even more determined to put a special effort into the garden and as spring was not far away, I spent the occasional day outside attacking what was a near wilderness.

Although the front garden was small there was evidence that it had been a very pretty patch at one time. My aim was to restore the garden area to the state it must have been in a few years earlier rather than to change it in any way. My reasons were based on the belief that the last owner had been an enthusiastic and expert gardener. This was later confirmed by neighbours who said that before she became ill she spent most of her time in the garden and that she was something of a plant collector. My determination was therefore to proceed with the utmost caution and, as we were now well into February, a number of things were springing into life and many of the bulbs were showing through the undergrowth, a mixture of ground cover plants and matted weeds.

A feature of the front of the house was a low wall covered in trailing or climbing subjects and it was looking at its worst in February – brown, dry and untidy. The temptation was to pull it all off and start with a clean wall but this I resisted, for to clad it again with new plants would have led to a long period with a bare wall. In any case at the end near the front gate there was a well established Virginia Creeper. Apart from a little trimming here and there I left well alone, concentrating my attentions on the beds at the foot of the wall and on either side of the gate outside.

On the right of the front door stood a medium-sized Laburnum which was really in the wrong place but would have to be left and trimmed slightly or taken away altogether. I opted to leave it for I need a very good reason to remove a tree. In due course, looking ahead a few years, it would have to come down but not until then. On the left of the door the wall was covered with a Cotoneaster which had wandered all over the place and in several places had come away from its moorings, but I decided again to leave well alone for the time being in order to see how it looked when the berries appeared. The temptation was to spend most of the time in the garden as the daylight hours extended but this was not possible and I concentrated again on work inside.

Two major tasks were now impinging on my plans. One, attention to the electrics all through the cottage, and two, the possibility of installing central heating. I knew I could not undertake anything myself concerned

The front door

with electricity other than the most elementary tasks and this meant calling in a contractor. As I had never had any experience of having a whole house rewired I was completely in the dark as to the sort of cost that might be involved and I knew of no one who could give me independent advice. In the event I stumbled on a solution to the first part of the problem of obtaining an estimate. I had seen a young man passing the cottage regularly to and from College Farm. One day I noticed that he was carrying a coil of electric cable and it became obvious that he was involved in electrical work at the house and buildings. I enquired tactfully of my neighbour Austin who willingly told me that some rewiring was being done and that he had engaged Paul to do it. He said that the workmanship was good and that he got on with the job as promised and further that Paul's charges were reasonable.

It seemed sensible to ask Paul, who lived in the village, to come and have a look at the work needing to be done and this he promised to do one evening soon. We eventually agreed a date and time which was after my evening meal. Although when I had seen him about the village, I had formed an impression of a rather casual sort of person, when we came face to face, I took an immediate liking to him. He did not try to impress but approached the encounter with a very light touch. He had a very sharp mind and a ready wit which made our meeting a very pleasant one. We moved round the house and I held the end of the tape whilst he took measurements. In one or two places he made suggestions as to how the positioning of switches and outlets could be improved and his whole attention was given to my needs rather than his own ideas of what these might be.

We returned to the sitting room and I offered him a beer. I assumed that he would take the details home and then submit an estimate but to my surprise he said he would give me an estimate there and then if he were given a little time to make his calculations. As he worked at the figures he confirmed one or two points on which he had given me options and I made decisions on these. He then said that I should hold tight to my chair whilst he spelled out the figure. I had been much impressed by his whole approach to the exercise and this, added to the fact that he lived in the village, had persuaded me to ask him to undertake the work providing the estimate was reasonable. I felt that if the figure was over £1,000 I would have to look for an alternative estimate. It would be difficult to justify my logic in setting such a limit for apart from one or two light fittings everything would be new including yards and yards of cable. His estimate was £750 with one condition, and that was that he would need payment at various stages in the work to enable him to purchase materials. In making my decision I had a rough benchmark to work to, namely the bathroom. This was going to cost £800 and the time taken would be far less than the rewiring. I had no hesitation in asking Paul to proceed with the work. He promised me that I would be next on the list when he had completed the work for Austin.

For the second time I had every reason to be pleased about a contract, for I was sure that I was not being overcharged nor was I taking advantage. I was also sure that the plumber and now Paul were the right men to take on the work. I had had considerable experience in managing men and resources and was certain that both men would do a first-class job. I was also convinced that I would find their company in the cottage very acceptable.

This encounter with Paul turned out to be the beginning of something quite important for he became my right-hand man as the renovation project developed and at times advisor *extraordinaire* on a whole range of matters. I shall be eternally grateful for the contribution he made during an important period of my life. He was married with four boys and lived in the village and was very much his own man. He had a multitude of skills and know-how, was very strong and above all highly energetic. Most important of all was the sense of enjoyment and satisfaction he derived from anything he did. If challenged by a new situation he would always contend that there was no problem and invariably this turned out to be true.

With these two large projects on the horizon, the garden springing into life and the cottage becoming more comfortable by the day, I now felt certain that choosing to come to Overdale was absolutely right.

Chapter eight

DISCOVERING THE GARDEN

Since my arrival at Overdale with the furniture, time was speeding by almost unnoticed for so much was happening and there was an urgency to get things reasonably tidy. I needed to return to Eltisley, for, in line with common practice, I felt I ought to clean the house after the general upheaval of packing and moving. I also had some long-standing engagements I must keep and one or two events I hoped to be able to share with Brenda. I had been invited to stay for the weekend at Brenda's and staying there would be most enjoyable and incentive enough to leave Overdale behind for a short spell.

I did not look forward to cleaning the empty house but it had to be done in the interests of good relations with the new owners. I started immediately upon my arrival in order to get the job out of the way for there were better things to do. I eventually shut the door behind me and made my way to Brenda's. On the Saturday we all went to the Arts Theatre in the afternoon where we saw a Gilbert and Sullivan performance by the Cambridge Amateur Operatic Society, always good value for money. Afterwards to the Pizza House where the girls in particular enjoyed themselves finding their way quite easily through what to me was a most complicated menu. Then home to a log fire. The lunch on Sunday was as usual most enjoyable followed in the afternoon by a walk across the green.

Brenda was on duty at the hospital on Monday and so I let myself out of the house and set off on my return to Overdale. As I travelled I began to feel that strong as the attraction was to get to Eltisley as often as possible, somehow or another it was not going to work out and perhaps I ought not to impose myself on Brenda's hospitality so frequently. I consoled myself by thinking that time might bring a solution and that in any case I must give my full attention to Overdale and see what happened.

It was good to get back and slip into the routine of work and it was no hardship to get up early, have a quick breakfast and take up the next job or continue with the one in hand. The signs of spring were everywhere and I felt how lucky I was to be where I was and particularly at this time of year.

March was fast approaching and I now had in mind that quite soon word would come that the plumber would want to start work on the bathroom and I must prepare for this. The room involved was somewhat cluttered with bedding and furniture, destined in time for other places, and this must be cleared. In effect it meant completing a job which was only half done. I was happy with the main bedroom and any further additions would spoil the effect. I had no option other than to complete the furnishing of what was to become the guest bedroom. There was not a great choice of places to put beds and furniture, particularly as this was to be the twin-bedded room. As I had adapted a built-in cupboard there was no call for a wardrobe. The one remaining wardrobe was already in the third bedroom, which was to become the bathroom, and I believed it could stay there as I thought it would not be in the way of the plumber. This did in fact turn out to be the case. Within a few hours the job was complete, with beds in place and two dressing tables allocated a place along with an attractive bedroom chair. The overall effect was very pleasing and I congratulated myself on my burgeoning skills in interior design. In truth it was all a lucky chance that everything combined to make an attractive room. The colour which I had used on the walls was chosen because I had a tin by me, which economic factor dictated that I should use. It was pure coincidence that it provided a good background for carpet, curtains and furnishings. Having now got it looking good I proceeded to spoil it by loading up the beds with the residue of items from the third room for which no place had been determined at this stage. Nevertheless this was a temporary arrangement only to be tolerated for a limited time. A sense of order was emerging and I was now ready for Operation Bathroom to commence whenever the call for action came from the plumber.

One thing in particular spurred me on and that was word from David and Mary Hill that they hoped to visit me in the near future en route for a weekend in Wales where they were to attend a congress. This was a family event and some of the children would be with them. They were coming in early March and it was good news in so many ways, not least that I would be able to provide hospitality to a family who had been so good to me in times of need, for theirs was an ever open door to me. Their projected visit called for a special effort on my part. Overdale must be clean, tidy and warm, and adequate to welcome guests for whom I had such a high regard.

The cellar

Apart from Paul and Anne and my brother-in-law Harry, they would be my first visitors. It was to be a red letter day.

The one room in the house which had received little attention was the so-called workshop on the ground floor. I referred to it earlier as the cellar which was perhaps a more apt description. Its only window was two feet square and of frosted glass letting in absolutely minimum light. If I had been a keen photographer it could have been converted into an ideal dark room, but my ambition was to make it into a study/bedroom. Looking at it then, such aspirations seemed farcical. The walls were in parts bare of plaster, at other points plaster had been replaced by cement rendering of dubious quality. At the end away from the door there was a set of rough wooden shelves built into an alcove in the wall. The electrics consisted of a power point which had fed a series of electric motors and lathes set on a gigantic bench but which left much to be desired by way of safety. Some of the cable leading in and out of it was supported by pieces of ancient binder-twine. The lathes had gone but the bench remained. The floor was part paving slabs, part concrete and at some points bare earth. Added to all this, there was a curious collection of cupboards, one of which was an ex-washstand of what appeared to be fumed oak, but on closer examination turned out to be grey paint.

I installed a strong light and set about clearing everything out as a first step. Much of the furniture and fittings would have their uses at some stage, and those which were easily transportable I transferred to the stable across the road. I had to take a big hammer to the bench and this was a marathon task. It consisted mainly of plank wood held together by four-inch nails. Sheer determination kept me going for until the room was empty I could not proceed. There were also one or two wood- and iron-working tools which I retrieved along with rusty nails, screws and washers whilst the residue was packed for collection by the refuse services. I decided that these should be put out for collection in small doses as I had my doubts about them being accepted in one large heap. The clearing out was followed by a vigorous brushing down of walls, ceiling and floor and it was at this juncture that I discovered the one part of the room which had real merit, namely the ceiling. The joists were exposed and they were bearing the original wide floorboards of the bedroom above (earmarked for the bathroom). Although none of the timbers were of high quality, I believed they were the originals and had not unduly deteriorated. The whole was covered in several layers of whitewash and it seemed apparent that with some effort this ceiling could become a small showpiece in the cottage and ideal for what I hoped the room might become, namely the study/bedroom. This was to become one of the many challenges ahead but would have to bide its time. It was at least now as clean as such a place could be at this stage although not one to show off to anyone except as a curio.

The time had come to take stock of progress for I believed I was coming to the end of phase one of my renovation plan. All the rooms were clean, and the main pieces of furniture had been set in place. Most but not all of the boxes had been emptied and shelves and cupboards filled. I had even hung some of the pictures and all the rooms now possessed curtains. Many of these had been left behind by the previous owners and after a wash had been rehung. They would serve for the time being although my ambition was to have deep red velvet curtains in all the ground floor rooms, an idea I subsequently abandoned when I studied prices.

The bedrooms were reasonably tidy and the main one in particular, which contained the best of the bedroom furniture, was in a state in which it could be used by guests without my having any feelings of shame. With guests in mind I had high hopes that soon the bathroom would be installed for it was a considerable journey to the shower facilities below. In fact they were at the farthest possible point away from the bedrooms.

It seemed sensible now to do the minimum of work indoors and when the weather was favourable to work on jobs outside. There was still some indoor decoration to do but this could wait upon wet days and so I worked steadily on the borders outside the front gate and the ones inside the wall in front of the house. These were the ones which would be seen first by visitors to the house and although the work was tedious it was straightforward and I could see a distinct improvement in the borders as I worked. Care had to be taken for seedlings were beginning to appear at a stage when, in a garden which is unfamiliar, they can easily be mistaken for weeds.

I discovered a delicate blue flower poking through the undergrowth at the base of the front wall of the house, and within a few days more followed to make a patch of colour at a most unexpected time. This was new to me but a reference to my copy of *The Book of Garden Flowers*, by J. A. R. Phillips and J. Lupton (a book which every self-respecting gardener should not be without and in which the flower illustrations by Joan Lupton are as good as any to be found) I identified it as *Chionodoxa luciliae* or Glory of the Snow. This has its origins in the high altitudes of Crete and Asia Minor where it appears as the snow melts, which explains why it was doing so well in the garden at Overdale, a very exciting discovery. It seems to thrive best where it has the protection of ground cover providing it is not too dense. I have tried it in other places but it seems happiest in Cotswold country.

In the process of clearing I made the depressing discovery that many of the borders were being overwhelmed by Ground Elder, one of the largest and most persistent weeds. Eliminating it from this environment was going to be a formidable task for although some chemical treatment is possible in open ground, it is almost impossible in established borders. I had to take a philosophical view and convince myself that persistence would be rewarded. I have to confess that I am not an enthusiast for chemical weed control and this being so, I have to accept the pain of doing it the hard way. After intensive effort in the limited area of the front I had covered once, I saw a change, but I knew that it must not be long before I returned and went over it again. In the meantime I worked on the borders in the back garden near the rear of the house, again the first to be seen by visitors.

The back garden was conveniently divided into three distinct areas, the lower part being a terraced lawn with borders on three sides and a stone pathway on the left looking from the house. On the left of the pathway there was an area backed by a group of shrub roses which generally should not be pruned very often but which had been neglected to the point where they were very much intertwined with one another. Below this enclave there was a rock garden through which fell an artificial waterfall running down to a pond; artificial only in the sense that it had been fed not by a natural stream but by water which I believe came from a well above it.

The pond

None of the system was functional and at that time the pond was reliant on rainwater for its supply. I could see a lot of scope here, for at its best it must have been a very attractive feature of the property. At some stage this and the well would merit some attention.

Beyond these two areas, and separated by a trellis entrance clad by roses, was an area of herbaceous plants split by the pathway which led to a greenhouse. The overall length of the garden was 25 yards and the width nearest the house was 10 yards, narrowing to a width of 5 yards in the area of the greenhouse, the whole sloping gently towards the house. In addition to various shrubs there were three apple trees of advanced ages which had not been pruned for a number of years. I had no great hopes of these but would defer judgement until I saw how they cropped and what the quality of the fruit was like. As a first step I would take out as much dead wood as possible in the time available and as soon as I could get to it.

Across the road from the back garden there was a piece of land which could only be described as waste land. It was some 30 yards long and on average about 8 yards wide, and had become so wild and neglected that drastic treatment would be necessary. The same sort of treatment would also be required on another piece of land over the road in front of the house. This was irregular in shape but was approximately 20 yards by 15 yards. This piece contained the septic tank and when the tank had been installed, the soil excavated to accommodate it had been left beside it in a great big mound. Apart from being an eyesore, this detracted from the usefulness of the land. Something would need to be done with it and it was obvious that any solution would involve some hard graft or the cost of hiring a mechanical digger. However it would have to be deferred and it was low on my list of priorities.

On two sides of this piece of land there were a number of mature gooseberry bushes and near the road a row of raspberry canes. I would be able to assess the worth of all of these when they came to fruit and looked forward with some interest to this time. My guess was that this piece of land had been the vegetable and soft fruit garden but unfortunately it had been something of a dumping ground for tin cans, bicycle wheels, old pieces of metal and a tangled mess of steel wire, none of which was of any possible use. Taking a long view I believed I could steadily pass this through the refuse collection service in strong plastic bags, which I did with no angry feedback from the staff.

There was an enormous amount of work ahead to bring all these pieces of land under control but I had no doubt about my ability to accomplish this in due course, provided that I remained fit and well, and I would certainly enjoy doing it. I continued with my initial attack on the rear garden with a view to a second, more thorough going-over after a short period. In effect it was a bit like the painting of the Forth Bridge. By the time I had gone through it roughly in the first phase, I had to start again at the beginning. There were times when the weather drove me indoors but I discovered to my delight that the soil drained well and I got to work on it quite quickly after the rain had stopped. On the second time round the various seedlings had grown and were more easily recognisable. The soil was black and friable and easy to work. It was clear also that it was fertile, for once growth started, things shot up almost overnight.

One perennial which dominated many of the borders was *Geranium grandiflorum* or Cranesbill, and as this was quite an invader I thinned it out as I went along, although not as much as needed, as I learned when they all started to bloom. There was also a good collection of *Paeonia* (Peonies) which emerged, suddenly filling large areas with their deep coloured foliage followed by a profusion of dark pink blooms of excellent quality. The big excitement was the emergence of dozens of *Aquilegia* or Columbine plants in small colonies and in due course they displayed a wide range of colours and combinations of colours. I had to conclude that the former owner was particularly fond of them and allowed them the freedom of the garden. Another of her favourites must have been *Nepeta* or Catmint for this abounded particularly in the small borders outside the wall at the front.

The first colour of course was from the wide range of bulbs, amongst which were some unusually fine tulips. What was pleasing was that the previous owner had planted bulbs generously in the grass verges outside the house and along the roadside to very good effect. It meant that for a while there were some areas which could not be mown but the spring show of colour compensated well for this. Even now, with much work to be done in all corners of the land surrounding the house, Overdale was coming to life and presented a pretty countenance.

I had a telephone call from Mary Hill from Eltisley to say that they were travelling to Wales on Saturday 10th March and would like to call in on me on the way. This was exciting news for they would be my first visitors. I insisted they should stay for lunch. Planning for their visit preoccupied me for the few days before their arrival. There were two aspects to consider, one was the lunch menu and the other was to make sure that the house was clean, presentable and warm enough to welcome my first guests. I set aside three days to concentrate on these preparations and that included my shopping trip to Cheltenham which had now become a fixed event on the Friday of each week.

The first thing I did was to clean all the windows inside and out. Up until now I had continually put this off as it seemed a low priority job. I was quite amazed at the difference this simple act made to the appearance of the cottage, both outside looking in and inside looking out. It was almost like wearing spectacles for the first time when everything is in greater relief and colours more intense. In the light of this improvement, it seemed sensible to wash the paintwork on doors and window frames. The areas had collected dust and grime from all the activities which had gone on and here again soap and water wrought another minor miracle.

There remained the normal domestic tasks of carpet sweeping and dusting. Some polishing would have improved the appearance of much of the furniture but I had to abandon such ideas as time ran out and I needed to concentrate on the matter of food. My solution was to make a visit to Marks and Spencers in Cheltenham. Their food department was quite special and I knew I would find a full range of prepared dishes which only required heating or in some cases light cooking. As I was buying these on Friday for eating on Saturday I felt this would be an ideal solution. It would have been foolhardy of me to experiment with my cooking on special guests. My culinary skills were so limited that I might risk losing good friends by attempting to use them. A careful look round the food department helped me to formulate a menu which I thought might appeal. It would be soup and rolls, pizza with salad followed by a sweet. I found all of these in quick time, but my problem was one of quantities. Not being well practised in estimating the quantities required, I tended to err on the side of providing more than enough, or so I thought.

By Saturday morning I was just about ready to receive my visitors with table set and the kitchen prepared for the limited amount of cooking to be started at the appropriate time. I believed that as it was only a question of following the instructions about the lengths of time for heating etc, it would not be a very exacting process and I kept my fingers crossed.

Mary, Angela, Belinda and Bruce arrived with apologies for the absence of David, whose commitments at the hospital had prevented him from getting away. This was a great disappointment to me but the presence of Mary and the children was quite a joy. They were all intrigued by the cottage and were keen to have a good look round, the children being particularly excited by the garden and the outbuildings. They spent some time exploring every nook and cranny for it was one of those experiences which children seem to get so much out of. It was the air of mystery and what they were going to discover next which absorbed them. Our sophisticated society seems to rob our children of a sense of wonder and excitement but here were children who were really excited. I was pleased by their reaction and it confirmed in my mind that I was not viewing my new environment through rose-coloured spectacles, but that it also captured the imagination of others.

Preparing a meal for presentation where some use of cooker and hot plates is needed, providing drinks and showing people round a house and garden all at one and the same time is not an easy task even for the most highly skilled hostess and host. In my case, with strict limitations on skills and experience it became difficult, but rescue was at hand for Mary insisted on helping and we had a most enjoyable little lunch party. The pleasing thing was that all the food was eaten although I wondered at the time whether I might have over-catered. Second helpings were much in demand proving beyond doubt that the food was enjoyed by all. This had been my big worry for it must be disheartening after all the preparations one makes, to find people not enjoying it.

They took their leave and went joyfully on their way leaving me with a good feeling inside that they had enjoyed their brief visit. What more could I have wished for?

During the week which followed things really began to happen with the arrival of the plumber and his apprentice, intent on installing the bathroom suite and all the attendant pipework. On receiving word of his arrival, some days earlier I had telephoned the building suppliers with a request to deliver the suite as ordered and true to their word it arrived on the morning of the plumber's appearance. The plumber obviously had a well-conceived plan of action, often difficult for the lay person to understand, but they were soon hard at work, calling on me occasionally when the positioning of the toilet, bath and wash basin were being decided. The approximate positions had been agreed when he first looked at the job but fine tuning was required. The first and most difficult operation was making the hole in the wall where the soil pipe was to enter the room on the outside wall. This proved to be a considerable challenge, although not a new experience for the plumber who was accustomed to working in buildings with Cotswold stone walls which, like those of Overdale, would often be 24 inches thick.

By mid-afternoon, he had broken through and it was downhill all the way after that in more senses than one. By the time he packed up for the night the soil pipe was through the wall and had been extended along the gable end on its way to the drain to which it would be connected. As all the water services were already located in the bedroom to serve the hot water system, it was child's play when these were picked up and laid to the taps in bath, toilet and wash basin. The remaining task was connecting the soil pipe to the existing sewage pipe and this involved the digging of a small trench outside the back door.

At the end of the third day, the job was complete and the place was ready to use. The next morning I was able to luxuriate in a hot bath in my own luxury bathroom giving me illusions of grandeur which proved of only a temporary nature. All this at a total of £809 and zero VAT. Suddenly Overdale had stepped into the twentieth century with its shower room, toilet and wash basin on the ground floor and a luxury bathroom on the first floor, probably the only small cottage in the village with dual facilities.

Observing the plumber at work and seeing the quality and speed of it, I decided that I could not do better than to get him to give me an estimate for the installation of central heating for which he was well qualified. In addition to an apprenticeship qualification as a plumber he had taken an intensive City and Guilds course in the science of domestic heating systems, culminating in a recognised qualification, all of which became evident when he came to plan my central heating system.

The first step was to decide on the location and size of the radiators in each room and in passageways and landing, all of which he did in consultation with me, explaining the technicalities as we went. A total of ten radiators were recommended and I agreed this number. As there was no gas in the village the only option was an oil-fired boiler unit and on this point he had some very firm ideas. He could now calculate the size of the boiler required, dictated by the number and size of radiators, and was willing to advise on the best possible make of boiler to fulfil this requirement. His reasons for being very specific about the make of boiler were practical ones based on experience. He affirmed that his recommendation was the one which had been the most reliable of all the ones he had installed. As this was the most costly part of the installation, his guidance was valuable and I accepted it although the cost was to be about £800. We discussed at some length the question of the oil storage tank. His first suggestion was that it should be located in the corner of the garden furthest from the road but near the house, but to my surprise when I expressed doubts about this, for it was to be a tank 6 feet long, 6 feet in depth and 4 feet high, he said that it could be put at the top of the garden and be partially hidden by an existing tree. Although he was quite a young man, he was nonetheless sensitive to the environmental factors involved in an operation such as this, and was amenable to finding practical solutions. He assured me that the difference in cost would be minimal and that the armoured feed pipe would be installed underground from the tank to the house. This was all a great relief for a big green tank alongside the house would have been a permanent eyesore.

A few years before this, I had had experience of a modified central heating system being installed in the house at Eltisley, adding to the small system already there, and converting from a back boiler gravity feed installation to a solid fuel boiler and pump. With this experience behind me I believed I was able to assess the suitability of this estimate when it was to hand, and when it arrived within a few days I had no difficulty in accepting an estimate of £2,750, asking him to proceed with the job as soon as possible. My quick acceptance enabled him to put in an order for the boiler which would be the controlling factor in the starting date.

So much was happening at Overdale that my links with Eltisley were becoming less strong but I was most anxious that they should not be severed completely. I occasionally telephoned Brenda hoping that I could find a good reason for making a visit, but for the time being no reason emerged. As the installation of central heating was imminent and as at any time Paul the electrician might be starting the rewiring I had plenty on my mind. My personal affairs would have to wait.

Chapter nine

BACK TO SQUARE ONE

Although following the installation of the bathroom there was a relative lull in feverish activity, something always seemed to be happening. One morning I was looking out of the window when I noticed a couple of young men looking up at my chimney. This roused my curiosity, although only for a moment or two as they were knocking at the front door. They asked me whether I realised that the chimney and tiles around it needed some attention. I went out into the road to survey the focus of their interest which gave them the opportunity of explaining the extent of my problem. They said that the coping stones were loose and that the first four or five courses of brick needed pointing, along with the tiles around the bottom of the chimney. I have to admit that from the ground there did not appear to be much of a problem, but they persevered and the one who appeared to be the leader insisted on us taking a look from the rear of the house. I could detect some shortage of mortar at the back and I felt convinced that he had a point, and asked him to give me an estimate for the work he felt should be done. After some consideration he declared that it would not be more than £90 but could be less depending on what he found when he got up there. I knew that most builders would need scaffolding for such a job and that under any circumstances £90 was very cheap. I said he had better do the job and he promised to come the next day when he had completed a similar job for a near neighbour.

The next day the gang of four arrived complete with a long ladder and a short one, a bucket, sand and cement and mason's trowels. It seemed a very large party for such a small job but when things started they all had their distinct roles to play. Their leader, the young man who had canvassed the job, took command and there was much shouting and allocation of tasks, all on a very amicable note. Ladders were fixed, mortar mixed and the leader was aloft reporting to the support staff below. He chipped away at the mortar and made good preparation for the pointing operation. Unfortunately they were to cause some offence to my neighbour Austin, during which I kept well out of the way. He wanted to come out of his driveway on to the road in his car and needed to pass in front of Overdale. His rightful passage was blocked by the long ladder which reached to the eaves of the house and was then tied on to the short ladder running up to the chimney. There was a considerable performance unscrambling all this superstructure during which Austin, understandably, became somewhat impatient, berating the gang for causing such inconvenience. Although I could not hear much of the frenzied conversation, I think the gang retaliated in the vernacular and tempers became somewhat frayed.

In due course to my great relief they completed the job and I became rather anxious that they should leave the site before Austin's return. The whole episode was quite bizarre for I think there was only one skilled man served by three of the most curious labourers one could imagine. As far as I could detect from their behaviour, none had had any training in ladder work nor in any other building skills, but they were pleasant and possessed a sense of humour which seemed to knit them together as a team. Perhaps they dreamed of becoming another organisation like McAlpines, and I hoped they might. Their leader asked for £95 and I gladly paid him for they spent several hours on the job doing what was necessary. Who knows, their vigilance and perseverance might well have saved me hundreds of pounds if the conditions on the roof had deteriorated. I kept them well in mind as it was just possible I might need the services of such a group at a later date.

The next day saw the arrival of the central heating engineer along with a van full of pipes and radiators and a promise that the boiler unit was on its way. From the beginning it was obvious that I had not overestimated his level of skill and experience, for what appeared to me to be a very difficult operation in a house of the age of Overdale seemed child's play to him. By the time he packed up at the end of that day he had fixed all the radiators to the walls on the ground floor and some associated pipework. Wherever possible he was hiding the pipework but there were several places where this was not possible. In the event exposed copper pipe did not seem out of place in this old house. The following day the boiler arrived, but despite its weight it seemed a simple enough operation to set it in place on a plinth which he laid down in one corner of the study/bedroom. He had to leave the job at one point to attend to an emergency call which had cropped up suddenly but he was back with only a gap of a day and he then continued on to completion.

Towards the end the large black oil storage tank arrived on the back of a huge lorry and it struck me immediately that there was going to be a considerable problem in getting it from the lorry to the place where it was to be installed. There was no lifting gear and there was no access wide enough to get the lorry into the top end of the garden. The nearest unloading point was over a three-foot wall and from there it could be rolled. The heating engineer asked the driver to pull up as close as he could and then set off down the road towards the centre of the village. He returned within ten minutes accompanied by a small group of men who had been gently persuaded to come and lend a hand. He knew one or two of them and the others had been recruited by the ones he knew, or so I presumed. There were six of us in all and moving the tank suddenly became a simple matter. On the word of command we edged it off the lorry and from there rested it on top of the wall. The team dispersed to the garden side of the wall and we then carried the tank to within a few feet of its final resting place. I was most profuse in my thanks to all concerned for although I had not made the arrangements, I felt I had a moral responsibility for the movement of the tank; after all, I was the owner of the monster. Everyone seemed very jovial about it and I found it refreshing that total strangers should be willing to come and help. If such a thing had happened in certain communities, it would have required a couple of committee meetings followed by a working party before even a decision had been taken, let alone any action. Such are the advantages of a small community.

With boiler and tank now to hand the job would not be too long to completion and I thought it wise to go in search of an oil supplier. This was important as the system would have to be tested before the engineer left the site in case any adjustments were needed. By good fortune there was a small oil depot at Andoversford who were said to be quite competitive and efficient and so it proved to be. No doubt they too were pleased to meet a customer with an empty 500 gallon oil tank and promised to deliver within 12 hours' notice. This was an ideal arrangement as the engineer could not give an exact time when the tank would be ready to accept the fuel, but during the next few days the internal pipework was completed and connected to the boiler and the roof space was invaded to accommodate cold storage and expansion tanks.

As soon as the oil tank was on site the young man called in his father (and business partner) to help build plinths to lift the tank from the ground, and when these were set hard the tank was rolled up planks into position.

The remaining major task was the digging of a trench from the tank to the house to take the supply pipe, partly to hide it but more importantly to keep it safe from the frost. This was a job which called for assistance from the apprentice, who seemed to enjoy the challenge.

On 5th April the system was activated – this was an exciting moment for me and worth every penny of the £2,909 I paid for it. From now on, every last corner of the cottage would be made warm and comfortable. I had absolutely no doubt that the value of the house was enhanced by at least £5,000 and probably more if at some stage I decided to sell it. It was most pleasing to think that my £3,000 investment had increased overnight to £5,000, but above all the comfort it would bring to Overdale was immeasurably more important. It would also help in reducing my fuel bills for, as I said earlier, the sole source of heating had been electricity. I had kept records of my fuel consumption to date and within a few weeks I became convinced that my hopes for a dramatic fall in fuel costs would be realised; there was an oil gauge on the tank which enabled me to calculate consumption quite accurately.

The boiler possessed very sophisticated controls which were explained very clearly by the engineer and in addition he handed me a comprehensive instruction manual which was unusually clear. Each radiator had its own thermostat so that I now had a complete system which gave me many permutations to meet a wide range of conditions. It was a long time before the novelty of this fingertip control wore off, and during that time I used all the subtle changes available in the system as if it were a new toy.

As spring was now upon us the full use of the system was becoming unnecessary but during the following winter it came into its own, providing an ambient temperature of 70°F in all parts of the house where needed. Of all the days which were worthy of special mention, 5th April 1984 when the boiler was switched on was surely the most significant.

To date I had spent a total of £4,793 on improvements, and considering the transformation which had taken place it seemed a modest amount. The place was damp proof, I had a virtually new kitchen, a new luxury bathroom and a central heating system second to none, with the additional luxury of a wood burning stove. The cottage had now taken on a lived-in look and I had even gone so far as polishing the stone flags in the sitting room which were beginning to take on a most attractive warm stone colour instead of the mildewed look they displayed when first uncovered. There were pictures on the walls, books on the shelves and pretty pieces of china in all kinds of places. It was nearing the point when I could confidently invite guests to come and stay, all except for the fact that the electrical rewiring must be imminent. I had seen Paul about the village who promised he would be with me shortly and on 12th April he started operations with a bang. It was obvious he was going to make a big impact on the situation and he surely did.

He was a tall young man of athletic build but carrying no surplus weight. His athleticism was amply demonstrated as he went about his work, clinging on to the slightest protrusion rather than waste any time moving and positioning his ladder. On the roof or on a ladder, he moved about like a cat and with the ease and grace of a ballet dancer, appearing not to know the meaning of fear. He was dextrous and quick with an ability to analyse a problem and find a solution. In a house like Overdale there were no standard situations and each new piece of wiring provided Paul with a new challenge; after examining the situation, he would declare that there was no problem. For a while I kept my fingers crossed, for I felt sure his approach was so flamboyant that sooner or later he must come unstuck. It would not have surprised me to see him lying flat out at the bottom of a ladder. My anxiety quickly evaporated and my confidence in his ability grew into admiration. Here was the man for me, the one who could solve all my problems, at least on the electrical front, and for a few days all went well. This proved to be the calm before the storm. He had been working downstairs for the first period and then he made a start upstairs. It was at this point that he sought me out where I was working in the garden to tell me that he had some news for me. He had the knack of giving one bad news in a jocular fashion so that things never seemed as bad as they really were. In taking up the floorboards in the main bedroom he had made a strange discovery. The original floorboards had been overlaid with thin tongue and groove floorboards and many of these were in poor condition. What was infinitely worse was that the original boards below these were in an advanced state of decay, mainly as a result of woodworm infestation. His advice was that there was no alternative other than to remove all the timber and put in new floors. On examining the other bedrooms we found that the middle room and half the landing area suffered from the same problem. The bathroom with a single covering of broad elm boards was thankfully in good condition. Having agreed that all the rotten timber should be removed, we discussed what should be done by way of replacement. The cost of using floorboards was frightening and their use would involve considerable labour costs. Although it was sacrilege to contemplate it, the only alternative was to use large sheets of chipboard. This was now an acceptable method in common use in building modern houses and I was convinced that I had no option. Paul was fully in favour of this being done and in fact said that he would be willing to undertake the work immediately. His offer to do the job tipped the scales for me and I asked him to proceed.

When he said immediately, he really meant it and within an hour a huge pile of floorboards in various stages of decay was forming on top of a flower bed under the bedroom window where they had been dropped. Great clouds of dust were floating everywhere for Paul had called on the services of his next door neighbour who often worked with him and together they set about the job with gusto. I made feeble attempts to cover up some of the furniture and managed to dismantle the beds but they could not really wait for such refinements. I just resigned myself to the fact that things were going to get very dusty. The heavy items of furniture were left stranded on islands of board to be taken up when new floors were installed. We carried one of the single beds into the sitting room below because there was no possibility that I could sleep upstairs amongst the debris.

At the end of that day we had cleared the old timber from both bedrooms and Paul had ordered the necessary chipboard by phone, promised for delivery the next day. Taking up the boards had revealed a thick layer of dust and some rubble which had accumulated on top of the lath and plaster of the ceiling below. On examination the exposed joists proved not to be infested by woodworm as I had feared but we agreed that a dressing of anti-woodworm fluid would be a wise precaution.

We could not contemplate leaving the rubble and dust to be covered up by the new floors and so we all set about cleaning it. The larger pieces were shovelled out into buckets and then into plastic fertiliser bags for onward transmission to the top of the garden. The rest was taken up by way of a cylinder vacuum cleaner. It was a long and tedious, not to say dirty, process which I continued on my own when the new flooring arrived. I had to make a special trip to Cheltenham for a new supply of vacuum bags for they could only be reused once before they had to be scrapped. Paul and his mate dressed the joists and then started to lay the new floor. The task became easier once the first sheet of board was laid for it was then possible to move some of the furniture on to it thus allowing more room for further laying to take place.

Throughout the chaos which ensued from this terrific upheaval, Paul displayed his fine sense of humour and this helped us all to keep fairly composed. His philosophy, like mine, was to tackle a problem head on. Wringing the hands and hoping it will go away makes things worse, whereas taking swift action starts one on the road to overcoming it. Paul's account for renewing the floors (two bedrooms and part of the landing) was £240 which included all materials. I was more than pleased that he volunteered to do it and the price was very acceptable.

Work on the electrical wiring continued but there were one or two delays when Paul was called to other work. Another young man arrived on site one morning, a friend of Paul's who had come to stay for a short holiday. He was also an electrician. At this point Paul began to get fretful because the job was not getting finished as quickly as he would have wished. I think he was concerned that he might be holding up other things I might wish to do. As they sat eating their snack lunch one day, they called for me and asked if I had any objections to them working through the night in order to finish the job. It struck me as being a most curious request but I had no grounds for saying no. I didn't believe I would get much sleep with hammers going all night but I would have to accept that.

I was still sleeping downstairs and turned in at about 11 o'clock to the noise of hammering and chattering but I fell asleep in due course and slept well until about 6 o'clock. The house was strangely quiet and it was obvious that they had gone home to bed having completed the job. Although the rewiring had been completed very satisfactorily and now new floors installed, my feelings when I surveyed the whole scene in daylight were distinctly mixed for I saw a picture of total devastation. There was a thick layer of dust literally everywhere. Nothing had escaped. The floors, the walls and the furniture had turned a dull battleship grey. Nothing was in its proper place and moving about the house was akin to a major obstacle course. This was nothing to do with the work during the night but an accumulation over the period when the work was progressing. It was only now when work had stopped and the house was quiet that the scene made its full impact on me, but as I thought back to how clean, tidy and attractive it had been before this operation started, I blamed no one, for none of it could have been avoided. Once we encountered the floorboard problem no steps could have been taken to avoid the results now visible. It simply meant that I must get round to bringing some order out of chaos and it would take time and effort, both of which were free and in plentiful supply.

One of the worst problems was the huge stack of decaying floorboards outside the diningroom window. It could not possibly have been built in a worse place for it was in full view of the village green and on the side of the road frequently used by people walking out from the village, as they did with their dogs or visitors. Naturally Paul made a great joke of my predicament which was perhaps the best attitude to take but my problem was one of extreme embarrassment. The whole thing was a dreadful eyesore and, particularly because it was a pile rather than a stack, an ideal collection for 5th November which was some six months away. It was all so tightly knitted together and in such quantity that restacking it tidily was out of the question. It could not be forgotten but as the days went by it became less obtrusive to me. My energies were being invested in the major clean-up programme, for there was no comfort anywhere in the house.

The first priority was the kitchen, for I had to eat and getting the place clean and hygienic again was critical. At a time like this I realised how valuable a vacuum cleaner was. To contemplate cleaning up this sort of accumulation with a hand brush and dustpan was quite mind-boggling although before vacuum cleaners were available on a mass scale people would have had to do just that. The problem in that method was that only a proportion was picked up and the rest moved along for further collection. Once round with the vacuum cleaner and you are nine-tenths of the way to completing the job. The amount of dust, grit and rubble meant frequent emptying of bags, but this was a small hardship to endure alongside the dent I was making on the problem.

It is often said that if you leave a problem alone it will sometimes solve itself and this was my tendency with the pile of wood. I just refused to think about it until one day out of the blue the solution was presented to me on a plate and I found it difficult to believe that I could have such luck. The heating engineer paid me a visit to make an adjustment to the boiler and, seeing the pile of wood outside, he enquired as to whether I might want to sell it. He said that he had a large woodburning stove which was in constant need of stoking and this wood would be ideal for the job. I had never thought it possible that anyone would want to buy it, rather I had been thinking how much it might cost to have it carted away. When I said I would be willing to sell it, he then wanted to know what I might charge. I had absolutely no idea of its value and I stated a figure from the top of my head on the basis of his willingness to buy it. I wondered if £10 would be reasonable and without hesitation he affirmed that that would suit him well. In five minutes flat the problem was solved. I had to wait some little time before it was moved but when he came he approached the job in the same efficient way he did everything else. He took every last piece leaving the site absolutely clean.

Having at last restored the whole house to its original state before the holocaust I could turn my attention to the next major work which was the development of the study/bedroom. I use the word development as renovation would not be appropriate. This was to be something new, for the room had been a workshop and had never been habitable. My aim was to bring it into use as a study/bedroom which I could use to sleep in myself when I entertained more than two guests. Three major tasks were required. One, the walls needed plastering, two, a window was essential, and three, a new floor would have to be laid. The obvious place for the window was in the front wall where the shelves were situated. One advantage of this location was that the shelves were recessed and as a result this was the easiest place to break through.

It occurred to me that the young man and his team who had renovated the chimney might be interested in this project for making a hole in the wall, for the window would be within their capability and possibly the plaster work. I rang him and he expressed an interest, agreeing to come and see me at the weekend. He arrived in the company of a lady who I discovered was his wife, and his friend who he announced was a skilled plasterer. They looked at the job and we discussed it together, the plasterer expressing some doubt about the standard of work he could produce in such hostile surroundings (my interpretation of the phrases he used to describe the primitive situation he saw). The walls were most curiously shaped, leaning out in some places and receding in others, somewhat like the surface of the moon. I imagine he had done most of his plastering on the new estates which had developed in and around Cheltenham and the contours of my walls were quite alien to him. The window seemed to present no problems and as there was a lintel in place at the right spot in the wall, the job seemed fairly straightforward. They gave me an approximate estimate, which I accepted, and agreed to start work the following weekend.

When they arrived I noticed that there had been a change of personnel in the team and the two replacements were younger men. Notwithstanding these changes they all went to work with a will. The leader used one of the young men as his labourer and the plasterer the other. There was a certain amount of chipping off to do on the walls where the plaster was loose, and then the first coat was applied. Breaking through the walls was much harder than they had expected and hand tools had to be abandoned in favour of a small pneumatic chisel but by the end of the day good progress had been made. The plasterer still complained slightly about the walls but I encouraged him by saying that it would suit me if he followed the natural contours of the walls within reason. I showed him several places in the cottage where the plaster work was far from square and upright and I think he got the message. As the initial plaster coat had to dry before he could apply the finishing coat, it was agreed that they would come the following Saturday to complete the job.

They had worked very hard on the window and it was not surprising that it was unfinished when they left. I felt sorry for them that their estimate had been set too low and in the interests of keeping them motivated I suggested that in fairness, I would not keep them to their fairly low figure. This worked well and they returned the following Saturday determined to finish the job and with a window frame to fill the gap when that point was reached. This was already glazed, a slightly unorthodox method, but in line with the revolutionary approach they applied to most of their work. They were big in the field of trial and error, exemplifying the saying 'if you never make mistakes, you never make anything'. I looked in from time to time and things were going very well. I was particularly struck by the concentration being shown by the plasterer and as I watched, it became clear that he had become highly motivated. I think he had taken up the challenge and was going to leave the mark of his craftsmanship behind. At the end he waxed quite lyrical about the room and there was no doubt that he was proud of the job he had done. He had worked with the shape of the walls and the room and had produced a fine piece of high quality work, absolutely in tune with the room and the rest of the house.

I commended them for the quality of the total job and also their determination to complete it quickly. I paid them £450 and felt again that I had spent money wisely. The study/bedroom was taking shape and the next phase was well within my capabilities and I was determined to make a start on this quite soon.

The next task towards completing the creation of the study/bedroom was to lay a new floor. This turned out to be much simpler than I had envisaged. I had been advised to try a new product recently brought on to the market. It consisted of a dry mix to which water had to be added, and it was then poured into place. As the area concerned was small, it turned out to be a very suitable method. I completed it in two stages by putting a single piece of shuttering across the centre of the area so that I could complete half of the floor in phase one. When this was set by the next morning,

I completed the second half in the same way. Not an absolutely perfect job but adequate for a first attempt.

One job remained, and that was to clean off the ceiling joists and then stain them in dark oak, finally putting two coats of white paint on the boards between them. This completed the transformation of the workshop into a study/bedroom and I was more than pleased with the final result.

Although there was no shortage of work to be done in the cottage, the time had come to concentrate some attention once more on the garden, for weeds and plants were growing fast, not to mention the grass. I also felt the need to expand my horizons beyond the house, which had absorbed and sometimes exhausted me for many weeks. My previous spell in the garden had set the pattern of work and I continued this, cleaning and weeding in a systematic way. Things were growing fast now which meant that unless I got on top of the job, I would lose the fight and weeds would dominate again. It was turning out to be an ideal spring of warm sunshine and occasional showers, and as I worked I began to absorb the environment in which I had chosen to live my life. From where I worked I could see the tops of the houses of the village which stretched out before me in front and to the side of the house. Occasionally someone would come by and most seemed anxious to introduce themselves. One of their main topics of conversation was an expression of their pleasure at seeing the old cottage come to life again after its long period of near dereliction. Many of them were keen gardeners and commented on the problem I was wrestling with. I had to confess to them that although I had a big job on my hands, it was giving me considerable pleasure.

The thing which gave me most enjoyment during this hectic period of my life was my visits to Paul and Anne at Milton. From time to time they telephoned me with an invitation to an evening meal. I could produce nothing to compare with the excellence of Anne's cooking and that, coupled with the welcome they gave me on each of my visits, meant I always came away fortified and revitalised for the days ahead.

In return I invited them to eat with me occasionally, making a special effort to provide something good, such as a roast or sometimes a steak. I could always rely on Anne rescuing me if things got hectic in the kitchen, or guiding me as the case might be. They were always interested in seeing all the work that had gone on since their last visit and I think they were happy that I was managing to get things done and enjoying it all.

Chapter ten

SPRING AND CELEBRATIONS

When Paul and his team had completed the rewiring project, he floated the idea that he and his helpers should take me out for a meal at the local pub one evening by way of celebration. At first I believed that this was one of his jokes but he mentioned it again and I could see he was really quite serious about it. My own feeling was that it ought to have been me taking them out and when I said I would like to join them but that the meal would be on me, he would not hear of it. A date was fixed and I was told to be ready at 8 o'clock with the additional instruction that dress would be informal. It was certainly informal as he had been out on a job and turned up in his working gear. I felt very much overdressed for the occasion but secure in the knowledge that as they were regular attenders at the pub they knew what was acceptable. They picked me up, announcing that there was some doubt as to whether Paul's car would actually get us there. It was the most unreliable vehicle imaginable and there had been many occasions when he had been called from work at Overdale to rescue his wife who had found herself stranded with a broken-down car. That night he took the view that should it break down there were enough of us to push. We tumbled out of the car and I brushed cement dust off my coat, following them into the pub and making an attempt to get to the front to buy the drinks. This was not to be; he said that the drinks and the food would be paid for out of the profit he had made on the rewiring of Overdale. I pointed out that this was no way to run a business but he brushed all my protests aside. The pub was full of people who appeared to be locals for they all knew Paul and for each one he had a merry quip. We did not drink to excess but the three young men did full justice to the food. Most of the dishes were 'something and chips', of which they had double portions. In my case it was a considerable struggle to consume it all which I felt I must, in order not to offend my host.

The conservatory

Paul had a serious side to his personality and although we had a good deal of fun, he did not forget that there were other things to think about. He went on to say that one of the reasons for the celebration was to get me out of Overdale for a while. He thought it was important for me to stop work and relax. He had learned of the recent happenings in my life from our conversation and was sensitive enough to realise that there were times when memories surfaced and clouds gathered, bringing phases of depression. I believe he saw a role for himself in this and in his wisdom concluded that support was what I needed. At the end of the evening he made it clear that they were pleased that I had accepted their invitation and expressed what a pleasure it had been to work at Overdale. I thanked them for their hospitality and at the same time made a point to Paul that if he had the time, there were a number of jobs I hoped he might do for me. I believe this was good news for him and he said he would visit me soon. Fortunately the car started at the first turn of the ignition and they dropped me at home.

Since my move in February the pace of work had been frenetic and as May approached it seemed to me that I needed to slow down or I might burn myself out. After all there was lots of time ahead. The cottage, inside at least, was clean, tidy and very presentable. The garden was no longer a wilderness although there was still enough work there alone to keep me busy for several weeks. I decided that the time had come to look for some relaxation. My memories of following the Yorkshire County Cricket Club round the country in the previous summer were still fresh and I believed it might be possible to repeat at least some of those experiences. The first matches of the John Player League were scheduled for early May and I decided that this would make a good start for me as Yorkshire were visiting Somerset at Taunton. I felt that this was quite a *local* event and that I should go. The fact that I saw it as a local event led me to think that I could move off about mid-morning and be there in ample time for the 2 o'clock start. Taunton seemed no distance and I was soon on the M5 motoring along comfortably at about 60 mph. It was about 12 o'clock when I began to take notice of the signs and saw Taunton – 70 miles. I realised then how stupid I had been and immediately stepped up my speed to 70 mph. It was too late to rectify my mistake and I knew I would not make the start of the match. The other annoying thing was that I set out to take a leisurely journey and here I was, putting myself under stress.

When I finally got to the ground Somerset were at the crease and going well. It was a fine day but fairly cool and there was an enthusiastic crowd for this was still the time when a visit of the Yorkshire team attracted extra spectators. Somerset made a reasonable score and Yorkshire opened as if they were playing a three-day match, with Boycott at his most defensive. The momentum increased after a while and Boycott began to attack the bowling with some uncharacteristically aggressive strokes. The game was now alive and then suddenly a lofted drive from Boycott went straight to the hands of the boundary fielder by the sight screen. That seemed to settle the matter and from then on Yorkshire were struggling and in the end lost the match. I returned to Overdale with the feeling that Yorkshire had made a poor start to the season.

The following day brought its compensations for the disappointment of Sunday, as I had a call from David and Mary Hill saying that they would like to take up my invitation to stay and would be able to come on the weekend of 12th May, arriving about lunch time on Saturday and returning on Sunday evening. This would be a very special occasion as David and Mary and the family would be my first guests to stay overnight. All my plans and activities for making Overdale a comfortable place would be put to the test as would my role as host. Mary urged me not to make too many plans as she would be bringing a certain amount of prepared food. We agreed various items on the phone and it was clear to me that with Mary's help the catering would not be too difficult.

I had asked Paul to come and have a look at the Conservatory (so called) at the back of the house for it was imperative that some action should be taken. It was a distinct eyesore and was also beginning to look dangerous. Apart from everything else it downgraded the whole appearance of Overdale. I expected that I would have visitors through the spring and summer and felt it should come down. The glazing bars were perished and the putty had gone to powder, to the point where renovation was going to be difficult. We discussed it together and concluded that it must be renewed. We also agreed that it would be best to renew it exactly as it was, the main point being that most of the glass was intact and could be reused. The cost of new glass would have been high at the thickness required and the existing glass was not too old. Paul suggested that I should pay for the materials and then pay him by the hour for the work of dismantling and erecting. From my point of view this was a most acceptable arrangement.

So began the demolition act, with great care being taken with extracting the glass and carefully stacking it, followed by a more aggressive attack on the half-rotten glazing bars. As Paul had other jobs in hand he was not a daily visitor but he came and went as he liked, which suited me. He had located glazing bars and the other timber at competitive prices and I paid for these as work progressed. Although his main skills were in the field of electricity, he was more than competent at carpentry work and in due course the skeleton of the conservatory was assembled. As carpentry is one of my own skills I knew the quality of the jointing was to a good standard and that the structure was going to be sturdy and safe. At this juncture he came up with the idea that it would be wise to clean and point the stone wall of the house above the conservatory before glazing was undertaken, and also to paint the outside of the landing window. At this stage it was possible to put ladders up to the wall from inside the skeleton of the conservatory and I quickly agreed that this should be done. The rest of the wall could be left to a later time. The cleaning and pointing of Cotswold stone walls is a difficult operation for all the stones are of different sizes and the depths of pointing vary greatly. He went off to seek advice and returned with a well worked out scheme which proved to be good although very messy for the craftsman. The mortar mix was quite thin and was pressed into the niches by hand. It was then brushed over with a damp brush. The small surplus left on the face of the stone was brushed off as it began to dry. I began to worry about how the whole thing would look when completely dry, but sure enough it was as he said it would be and quite acceptable. This was a long and tedious job and was spread over several days but was a definite improvement which when the whole wall was completed would look fine; and I also took the opportunity of painting the small window above.

The time was right now for completion of the conservatory, starting first with the painting of the glazing bars with primer, undercoat and gloss. When all was finally dry we came to the all-important job of glazing and this gave rise to debate. One area in which I had more knowledge and skill than Paul was glazing. Over the years I had undertaken quite a bit of this work, particularly one spell when I reglazed a whole moderately-sized greenhouse. The modern idea of greenhouse glazing by laying putty on the glazing bars, setting the glass in place and trimming the putty level with the upper surface of the glass was not a method he had used. After a careful demonstration he accepted that it was a good idea and completed the job using this method. When painted it brought a much enhanced appearance to the rear of the house. Paul was rightly proud of the completed job and was beginning to treat the house as if it were his own. He was full of suggestions as to how further improvements could be made and, considering the conservatory restoration had only cost £310, I was more than willing to listen to his suggestions but at the same time had to keep in mind available financial resources. I agreed that he should complete the pointing and cleaning of the back of the house and we would then review the situation. It was very reassuring to know that we could proceed on this basis and he in turn found it gave him freedom to take on jobs elsewhere as and when they came along.

As May unfolded the days got warmer and the Cotswolds were bathed in sunshine. The colours became daily more intense. So much blossom on the spring-flowering shrubs and the contrasting greens of the trees as leaves unfurled were a joy to see. Shipton Oliffe and Overdale itself played their part in this landscape although things were rushing ahead so fast that I had to take some action. The growth of grass was overwhelming me. I had been able to keep the small piece of grass in the front in check and likewise the formal lawn on the terrace at the back of the house with the Ransome electric mower which came with me from Eltisley, but in addition to these pieces there was a total of about half an acre including the grass verges on the road outside which was growing too fast for a cylinder mower and which in any case needed different treatment. The answer was to buy a rotary mower. It took no time at all to come to this decision and I was determined to deal with this on my weekly shopping visit to Cheltenham. Having laid in my weekly stock of food and loaded it into the car I found a most excellent mechanical tools business not many yards from the main shopping area. There were mowers outside in front of the shop and lots more inside. I had narrowed down my field of choice, deciding that it would need to be petrol-driven, as all the grass other than the lawns was too remote from the electrical supply in the house. It would also need to make a wider cut than my existing mower but not so wide that it could not be easily manoeuvred around trees and shrubs and over some fairly uneven terrain. The owner of the business was most attentive to my needs and showed me two or three, any of which would meet my requirements. I had had some experience with a Mountfield during my stay at Eltisley. My friend Michael Cropley and I used to spend a certain amount of our leisure time mowing corners of the large village green which could not be done by the gang mowers and we used a Mountfield which had been recommended by Michael. (Apropos of this, when I left the village Dr Stott the rector made special mention of my efforts in the Parish Magazine. I found it gratifying to know that I had been remembered in dispatches even if it was only for mowing grass.) It did not take me long to make up my mind that I should buy a Mountfield, particularly in the light of my recognised skill in using one. This machine would undoubtedly meet all my needs and it made a very up-market noise when at full power. At £143 it seemed absolutely right. I wrote out a cheque, went to get the car, loaded the mower into the back of the versatile Ford Fiesta and was soon back at Overdale eager to give the Mountfield a trial run.

After a speedy snack lunch I searched for my emergency petrol supply can, which in theory was supposed to live in the car. It was of course empty but this was no bad thing for 2 star petrol was strongly recommended for the Mountfield. A quick dash to the garage in the village of Andoversford was undertaken and then the filling completed. It had a pull start which for the uninitiated can be a little difficult. Providing you take care and follow the instructions all will be well. The pulling of the cord must be firm and deliberate and one must be aware that an engine can kick back. This is not unique to the Mountfield. All engines with a pull start behave in exactly the same way. My long experience in starting such equipment served me in good stead but it is true to say that every such machine has its own idiosyncracies. Know your mower is the key to success. I held my breath, foot on top of the mower casing and pulled the cord. Heaven be praised, it started first time with a full throaty roar which disturbed the peace and calm of the tiny village. I expected that at any moment I should have a visit from the local noise abatement society but nothing happened. Once it was throttled back it purred like a cat and on I went, up and down the grass verges feeling really pleased with myself that I had so quickly solved my problem. At the end of the afternoon, I had made quite an impression on the appearance of the environs of Overdale and I hoped people who walked by noticed the improvement. I did not have to wait long for an answer as several people commented favourably. I now knew that my investment was going to pay dividends over time.

I was now hurrying to do so much in the garden before the visit of David and Mary but at the same time knowing that I must reserve some time for final preparations in the house. The bulbs were over but other things provided colour, and in particular the numerous plants of Lungwort were dominating some of the borders with blue and pink flowers. This was partly as a result of neglect for it had become quite invasive and needed some thinning out. Even so, it now provided a most pleasant splash of colour, as did the blue of the Forget-Me-Nots, another invader. The Peonies were also coming to their best, mostly deep pink colours against their dark copper-coloured leaves, in contrast to some of the green foliage dotted throughout the borders. The bush roses, some of which were very old, were now coming into full leaf and even at this stage it seemed right to tidy them up rather than leave them straggling all over the place. I worked at this with some lack of confidence as I had neither the time nor the knowledge to do more.

I now switched my efforts indoors to prepare for the arrival of Mary and David, moving myself out of the main bedroom into the new but rather bare study/bedroom. Fortunately I had retained the third of the single beds, which I now set up and prepared the room for occupation. The main task was preparing beds, then the normal cleaning including a certain amount of polishing of furniture in the main bedroom. Everything had been subjected to so much dust and grit that polish was essential. In the twin room the furniture was of white and pink painted whitewood. I was able to bring out of safe keeping a number of trinkets, cameos and small ornaments, which had been obtained and used by Anne several years ago, and they gave the room a young female atmosphere, just right I thought for Angela and Belinda. I was pleased by the end result of my efforts and felt that they would feel comfortable in such surroundings. Above all they would be cosy and warm as a result of an effective central heating system. With easy access to the bathroom they would be in a self-contained family unit.

My final effort was to get everything looking at its best on the ground floor, and here again this was basically dusting and polishing, bringing things out of drawers to add to the ornaments I had placed earlier, all of which had been carefully collected over many years, such as china, glass and brassware. I carried out preparation for our meals as far as I could and now all was ready.

I had worked out a number of activities which we might undertake built round the theme of looking at the Cotswolds, with various options as alternatives. I kept in mind that it was important that there was plenty to interest the children.

They arrived on Saturday, 12th May in time for a snack lunch and after a thorough exploration of the cottage, for this was David's first visit, we loaded up into David's car and travelled gently through the countryside stopping at various points to view the superb landscape, probably just then at its best, and more so because of the magnificent sunny day. This was in fact the first time they had really explored the Cotswolds. We took the road to Winchcombe through Brockhampton and Charlton Abbots. In Brockhampton Park (then owned by the Dowty Group) we were fortunate in catching sight of the unique herd of white deer. We stopped at several vantage points as we descended the steep slopes into Winchcombe. The valley of the tiny river Isbourne, which joins the Avon at Evesham, stretched away into the distance with the medieaval Sudeley Castle in the foreground. A very nostalgic view for me as I spent several happy years with my family as Farm Bailiff at the Home Farm of the Sudeley Castle Estate.

We took a gentle stroll round the small town of Winchcombe with its magnificent wool church and its tudor inn, The George. The little town teems with Cotswold stone houses arranged along its narrow streets in their infinite variety, each with its own special identity and different to its neighbour. Why on earth we have to build our houses today each exactly like its neighbour I fail to understand. There are signs of a change but it is a weak effort. My visitors were all entranced by what they saw, expressing a wish to carry on. We took the Broadway road out of Winchcombe, turning off to Hailes Abbey. There we walked round the peaceful ruins set amongst the fertile orchard land which stretches all along this valley, then drove on to Santon and Stanway with their special charm, completely free from any ugly modern additions. From there we climbed Stanway Hill, famous for its Laburnums which line the road on either side as it winds to the summit; a wonderful sight when they are all in full bloom. We headed across the top through Naunton and home to Shipton Oliffe.

We had a leisurely meal and although it was not late Belinda and Angela thought they would like to go to bed. They had expressed some delight when they first saw their bedroom and when they had gone up Mary said this was the attraction, the novelty of a different bedroom. We made a concerted attack on the washing up and the evening of conversation flew by. We had all worked together in various organisations in the village of Eltisley and as I had been away now for a while we spent some of our time talking about what had been going on there. David was intent on rising early the next morning as he was going to drive to Buckinghamshire to pick up Bruce who had the day off from his boarding school and would spend it with us at Overdale. We were not late turning in and I got the impression that my guests had thoroughly enjoyed themselves.

I heard David about early next morning and got up immediately to make sure he had something to eat before he left. As usual he was determined not to put burdens on anyone and was foraging for himself, assuring me that he had everything he needed, and in due course he left on his journey to pick up Bruce. I was able to prepare breakfast for Mary and the girls in a leisurely fashion and eventually they all came down. Their needs were modest and my plans of cooking bacon and egg for everyone evaporated. Quite sensibly perhaps they took a very frugal breakfast.

David and Bruce were expected well ahead of lunch time and so with Mary's help I set about preparing Sunday lunch, roast beef and Yorkshire pudding with several vegetables, a menu I had been practising with on Paul and Anne and which seemed to work quite well. Mary had brought a prepared sweet. Her approach to cooking was slightly different to mine and I think she felt I made too much fuss about everything. I am sure she was right but my fussiness grew out of my anxiety to get everything just right whereas Mary had a more relaxed attitude to the whole thing. She also had a nice sense of humour, taking the view that we all probably took eating too seriously. It was a pleasant experience working with her in the kitchen – what might have been hard work turned into a great pleasure and I learned a few tips by watching Mary at work.

It was nice to welcome Bruce again to Overdale and he was obviously overjoyed to be with his family again. Like most children living away from home, it was a welcome break from a fairly spartan life at school. I was hopeful that we could make the day happy for him and I found him easy company as I did the girls; not always the case between young and old. He and all of us enjoyed the meal enormously and it only proved that my fussing had been totally unnecessary. Second helpings were not uncommon and we were well fortified.

My main plan for the rest of the day was a visit to the Cotswold Rare Breeds Park. I had been before and found it to be particularly interesting to children and animal lovers. I felt it would be ideal for our group and it was certainly accepted with some enthusiasm. For those who wish it, it is also a hands-on experience. There are special areas where the animals roam freely and can be handled, particularly goats and sheep. In other places animals can be seen living in natural conditions and many are quite rare. The owner, who is also a successful farmer, has accomplished great things there by preserving and multiplying breeds of farm animals which might well have suffered extinction but for his efforts. It is a very pleasant site and given reasonable weather well worth a visit. We were fortunate because it was a bright sunny day and quite warm. We spent a long time roaming about and the children had an enjoyable time, as they are all animal lovers. Most children relate easily to small animals, particularly lambs, young goats and calves and these children were no exception. Angela had her own pony at home and this section of the park was of special interest to her. So the place was full of children, our party amongst them, and no discordant note was heard, only laughter. As far as the animals were concerned, they too seemed to enjoy the constant attempts being made to rub their ears and hug their necks and in general accepted the children's demonstrations of affection. Like the children, the animals displayed their own individual personalities, some coy, some slightly mischievious and some totally submissive. Just a few showed a sturdy independence. We can all learn from animals and it is safe to say that not one of them is naturally malicious. They can develop such traits if they receive such treatment, but they are basically innocent and, truth to tell, so are children until or unless their environment changes them. Some of course are more susceptible to environmental influences than others, resulting from inherited tendencies, which naturally means that they are all individuals and must be thought of as such.

Although the girls were reluctant to leave the park we felt another small tour would round off the day and we made our way to the Slaughters and then took the back roads to Shipton. All good things come to an end and with more than two hours' drive in front of them, they left me at about seven o'clock. I was loath to let them go for it had been a wonderful weekend for me and I knew their departure would leave me with a feeling of some depression. I have written earlier of their kindness to me during the black days of spring 1983 and onwards from there we had grown very close and had spent some happy hours together. This weekend had renewed all those feelings and I wished they could have stayed longer. My reward from their visit was to feel how much they had enjoyed it. The children still retained the innocence and sense of wonder which is so good to see. There is a tendency these days for children to become quickly bored, and occasionally one hears them saying 'It's boring'. Not so with David and Mary's children, they enjoyed every minute. Confirmation of all this came in a letter from David which he wrote the day after their return. Remember he had returned to the busy scene of his work as consultant in a famous Cambridge hospital, but despite this he found time to write to me as follows:

Dear Clifford

What a lovely time we had with you at Overdale. Angela enjoyed it so much that she felt she was still on holiday and it lasted until Monday morning when she quite forgot that she had to go to school. Such is the spell cast by the Cotswolds, and we quite understand your desire to return there, especially with all the other happy memories that it holds for you. Thank you very much for all your hospitality and comfort of your new home. We appreciate very much all the consideration that you showed us in planning such a pleasant programme.

We had a good run home dropping Bruce back at school and arrived to find everything safe and sound.

Take care of yourself and we hope that you enjoy your own break in Devon and the cricket of course. We will keep in touch, and should you want to make a trip to Eltisley, we always have a spare bed and would love to see you.*

Thank you again and we send our love.

David

I read and reread this letter and it meant and still means a lot to me. It was important that they should have enjoyed their visit so much, for I owed them and still owe them a great debt of gratitude for all they have done for me. I am eternally grateful.

A few days later I drove up the Fosse Way to Grace Road, Leicester, where Yorkshire had a three day match. My practice was always to attend the first day for I then had a fifty–fifty chance of seeing Boycott opening the innings. If, on the other hand, Yorkshire had to field on that day, I could decide about attending on the second day at the end of day one. I

* I did not take this break in the end.

rarely attended on day three. I had a simple formula for such trips and after breakfast I prepared a picnic lunch of cheese sandwiches and a couple of tomatoes, two bananas and a flask of boiling water for tea-making, all stuffed into my little black canvas bag. I left Overdale in bright sunshine and was soon coasting along the Fosse Way to Leicester. This must be the straightest road in England and one of the most attractive. It is single carriageway and almost without gradients. It was at that time a quiet road and hardly used by commercial vehicles. When I left it on my way into the outskirts of Leicester, I was quite amazed how many miles I had covered and in so short a time. From then on my progress was only steady, partly because of traffic being heavier but also because I had to find my way to the ground. I began to appreciate how clever the Romans were in their road construction programme. They knew the value of a straight line.

This was my first visit to Grace Road and I was not disappointed. It is true to say that most county cricket grounds in England stand as oases in a desert of industrialisation, and this was no exception. Inside the ground was like being in another world; everything was clean, green and white and bathed in sunshine; a magnificent sight. It was also very peaceful and quiet, being so early in the season. Unfortunately it was not warm and I was glad that I had loaded my duffle coat. I had secured a place in the grass car park behind the sight screen opposite the pavilion and was able to return to the car at lunch break and tea and get out of the wind. Leicestershire batted first and by half an hour from stumps, were all out. Boycott and Moxon came in for the last few overs and survived to start the second day. This helped to persuade me to come on the second day when I was amply rewarded by a magnificent innings by Boycott and a good one by Moxon. By the end of the day, the match was evenly poised but I had decided that a day at home was essential. There were more important things to do than sit watching cricket, but only just a little more important.

Chapter eleven

ILLUSIONS OF GRANDEUR

After he had completed the cleaning and pointing of the rear wall of the cottage towards the end of May, I was obliged to tell Paul that I would have to wait a little while before seeking further help. It was really a question of money and I needed to build up my reserves a little before further expenditure. He listed a number of jobs which needed doing and I did not disagree. They were all necessary and I would do them as soon as I could. I did say there was one small job he could do at his convenience. Near the back gate and at the top of the stairs from the conservatory there was a pond which was eight feet in diameter and which received the waterfall which tumbled over the rocks from above, running from the area of the well. It was not fed by a spring but relied on rainwater. The depth of this gave me cause for concern. It was some three feet deep and was surrounded by a dwarf stone wall giving easy access to children. Paul himself had young children who occasionally visited him when he was at work at Overdale and the number of children visiting was likely to increase. Apart from everything else, the garden was not childproof and I had visions of a small child wandering in one day and being fascinated by the pond. I believed that Paul was the man to advise on this and sure enough, he came up with the simplest of answers which, although staring me in the face, had not occurred to me. He said the only sensible solution was to make the pond shallow enough so that it ceased to be a danger to children. He could do this by filling it with rubble and there was quite a bit of this to hand. He pointed out one or two large pieces lying about in various parts of the property, such as broken concrete blocks and broken bricks. It took him about half a day to collect the material, and one by one they were dropped into the pond which had a concrete bottom so that the water never drained away. From the large mound of soil dug out for the septic tank across the road, he retrieved a considerable amount of hardcore and wheeled it to the pond by the barrowload. The final ingredient was a layer of sand and soil. Not being an expert on ponds I was not too sure about the method used but he assured me that it would be fine. For many days afterwards the pond looked very gloomy, like thick soup, but in due course it cleared and the bottom could be seen. It was now about 18 inches deep and any child falling in would have no difficulty in climbing out. This problem had caused me concern for some time and had disturbed my sleep at times. I could now rest easy in my bed until something else cropped up to worry me.

For a while in the absence of Paul I had the place to myself and things seemed quiet. It was a welcome change although that implies no criticism of Paul. To some extent when he was there I had to work to some sort of schedule whereas now I could do exactly as I wished without reference to anyone. The weather was perfect as we moved gently into June, for the cooling winds of May had passed. It was so warm that during the day I could work wearing only shorts and as the place was now surrounded by shrubs and trees in full leaf, I felt I could do so without giving offence to anyone who might be passing. One rose bush after another burst into bloom and I was now able to make some attempt at identifying and naming them. The attempt proved somewhat abortive as I could find none of them in the books I possessed. As I pointed out earlier, the bulk of them were planted in a small area round the well and were quite old, and in the winter looked very untidy. Now, however, they came into their own, blooming in profusion one after another, at one point providing a riot of whites, pinks and reds, forming a spectacular background to that corner of the garden. There was a straggling climber clinging tenuously to the gable end of the house which despite its obvious age eventually produced large red blooms, but only sparsely. It would remain until time allowed for something better to be introduced. At the north end of the front garden there was the always reliable, strong growing Queen Elizabeth and nothing would stop that blooming. I had seen this popular variety in so many situations and it never ceased to amaze me. It always bloomed profusely and its leaves always looked shiny and healthy. The Laburnum outside the sitting room window, whose presence I had earlier questioned, did its best to prove that it had every right to stay by blooming abundantly, and I reserved my judgement on its future.

In several borders where I had cleared sufficient space, I had planted a number of Geraniums which I had brought from Eltisley and kept through the winter in the small lean-to greenhouse (a rather shabby affair) on the front of the house. These were now coming into bloom, adding quite a bit of colour to the borders. Although I was slightly ashamed of the greenhouse as it was quite an eyesore, it was invaluable for it was fitted with a thermostatically controlled heating system and had enabled me to keep some twenty or more parent plants through the winter; these would form the basis of my propagating plans for the coming autumn and for young cuttings. In due course I would be able to give attention to making the greenhouse more acceptable to look at.

The Columbines were doing their best to catch the eye and each day gave me a new surprise for there were all colours and combinations of colours in all parts of the garden, some in borders, some poking through the ground-cover plants, and everywhere else. Although there was much, much more to be done I felt that at this point I was on the way to a complete recovery of the garden, at least that part of it which surrounded the house.

The main greenhouse stood at the top of the garden and up to now I had tended to ignore it as a greenhouse, using it as a convenient storage space. It was soundly built and in good condition with a brick path down the centre and beds of soil on either side. It also had a substantial wooden staging on either side and a quite sophisticated set of greenhouse heating tubes served by electricity. The latter was a very late discovery but answered a question which I often asked myself about a junction box in the kitchen. This had been isolated when the rewiring was done as its destination was a mystery. In fact it was part of the supply system of electric power to a pump in the well (more of this later) and to the greenhouse and stone building at the top of the garden. Each of these discoveries demonstrated how efficient the whole place used to be in its heyday. Electric power was available in the most remote places. At this stage I had no plans to reactivate any of this but it had all come to light because of my more careful examination of the greenhouse. The other interesting discovery was that I possessed a vine. Its springing into life had been hidden under a heap of cardboard boxes and other material stuffed into the greenhouse waiting for the time when I could deal with them. I cleared everything away from the plant which was now making its way towards the light and, once given its freedom, it grew overnight and each day after. It had a clear requirement for lots of water which I soon satisfied, then I gave it a feed. As it grew I erected a wire frame to support it, believing that before long I might see some blossom and fruit. I waited and watched but apart from masses of shoots and leaves, nothing else appeared. I imagined that because I did not give the vine early attention when it started to grow, I reduced its chances of fruiting. I did little to help it during its growing period except provide support, partly from ignorance and partly because of lack of time. When it resolutely failed to fruit, I lost interest and, apart from an occasional watering, I ignored it, giving my attention to more important and urgent tasks. Having told people about my vine however, I lost a certain amount of face when I had to admit failure.

The more the sun shone the more energy I developed and I believed the time had come to spend a little time on the two plots of land on the edge of the property. Both presented me with the utmost foreboding for there were no short cuts to dealing with them. I made up my mind to do as much as I could with the piece in front of the house and if there was any time left, to make some effort with the piece on the side across the lane. I chose the front piece because it seemed that any effort expended there would begin to show almost immediately whereas the other piece had become so overgrown that the return for expenditure of energy there would be almost minimal. In any case it was surrounded by trees and shrubs, almost in full leaf now, which screened it from sight.

I had been thinking long and hard about what I should like to make of this front piece which, as I mentioned earlier, had a collection of soft fruits on the perimeters. Nearest to the house were raspberry canes, supported by a reasonably sound wire frame, and on the other sides, one of which was defined by a mature dividing hedge and the other by a wall, were a number of quite mature gooseberry bushes. It seemed sensible to allow all these to stay. In the corner near the entrance gate there were ten blackcurrant bushes which again I would leave to see how they yielded. The rest was open ground supporting an indifferent array of rough grasses which were now beginning to grow and which would soon be out of control. Sitting in the middle of this was the mountain of soil which had been dug out of the space which now housed the septic tank. Fortunately this mountain was at the top end of the sloping ground and it seemed that the sensible thing to do was to move the soil down the slope and fill the hollows below. Before starting this mammoth task, I decided to run the Mountfield mower over the grass, cutting it as low as I could in the circumstances. This is where I discovered a major hazard. I had gone but a few yards with the mower when there was a sickening whirring sound and the engine stalled. On examination I found that I had unearthed a piece of thick wire which was now partly wound around the blades of the mower. My first concern was for the well-being of the mower. I shuddered to think of the consequences which a broken-down mower would have for my plans, and but for the fact that it was the most robust machine, that would have been the case. Unfortunately the piece of wire was buried in the undergrowth and it took time and energy to detach it from where it lay buried and from around the blades. I now made a most careful examination of the ground only to find other pieces of wire, including one or two large rolls. The wire was not the only obstacle to progress, for further searching brought forth pieces of cast iron, an old bicycle frame, pram wheels, a steel window frame and some small oil drums in addition to other lengths of wire. In the end I conducted a systematic search of the ground and got together a substantial pile of scrap by the end of the day. This was piled in the corner near the exit until I could find a way of disposing of it. On the following day I was able to proceed with the initial mowing and I left the grass lying on the ground intending to burn it when dry.

I took a deep breath and mounted an attack on the mountain of earth, first by loading a wheelbarrow, wheeling it down the slope and tipping it in the hollows farthest away. It was a laborious process but I had a clear objective in mind and this spurred me on. If one is fit and able there is a certain joy in sheer hard physical work for its own sake and I was getting quite a kick out of this. I was more than encouraged when my neighbour Austin leaned over the wall and commented on the change I was making to the landscape. He said the mountain had been there for many years and had always been an eyesore to them. I knew now that my efforts were going to be worthwhile for not only would its removal please me, it would please my neighbours as well. At the end of the second day there was only a small amount of soil left to move and as luck would have it, this was the best soil in the heap. I would use this as the final topsoil on the area covered, and I scattered it evenly, finishing off by levelling it with a large garden rake. After leaving this to settle down my plan was to hoe it over, rake and roll it when the weeds had died back and ultimately to seed it down. What had appeared as a formidable task was now complete and I could make plans as to how to use the space. I could use part of it for a vegetable garden and perhaps extend the area of soft fruit, but this would add enormously to my work load, and what would I do with all the produce? In any case there were so many other things to occupy me, particularly in the main garden and around the house. I ruled out such ideas and decided to turn it into a shrubbery and perhaps at some stage erect a summer-house on it. The land faced south and caught the sun from morning till night. It was an ideal place for a swimming pool, and in a moment of fantasy I could see my friends gathering there on a summer afternoon and joining me in the pool. I feel fairly certain that this would really have upset my neighbours not to mention the planning authority. When I jokingly mentioned this idea to Paul and Anne, I could see from the look on their faces that they believed I was going out of my mind and exhibiting illusions of grandeur well beyond my means. The idea of a shrubbery and leisure corner took firm root in my mind and I sketched out a rough plan as to how it might finally look. This could be developed over time; in the meantime with the equipment at my disposal I could keep the place looking tidy. I scattered grass seed and hoped for some gentle showers and in due course the bare patches became greener and greener. Several people as they passed by on their walks commented favourably on the changes I had brought about. This was my best compensation and I felt I was being slowly accepted into the community of Shipton Oliffe.

The Mountfield mower was my constant companion for this was the time when the growth of grass was at its most vigorous. Having brought the land in front of the cottage under control and having tamed the grass verges alongside both roads, I had to keep up the good work. This meant the allocation of almost one day per week to mowing. It was undoubtedly time well spent for I could now cease to feel ashamed at the appearance of my property in comparison to those of my neighbours. One or two had expressed a wish to look round the garden. I hope they were not disappointed for I would not have claimed that it was any more than tidy. They did say that they often wondered what was behind those Cotswold stone walls and they certainly seemed intrigued by what they saw. One or two showed so much interest that I invited them to look over the house. I imagine they thought that after so much activity there must be something worth seeing. The thing I wanted to avoid was showing off, what after all, was only a modest little cottage.

I continued to hope that other friends would take up my invitation to join me at Overdale for a short stay, an invitation I always issued when speaking to them on the telephone; one day out of the blue I had a call from Valerie and Norman from Sheffield announcing that they would like to visit me on the next Saturday. I was excited at the prospect and tried to persuade them to stay overnight but commitments prevented this.

Someone who would travel from Sheffield to the Cotswolds and back in a day really demonstrated their desire to see me and I could not wait to see them. When they were first married, we were neighbours in Kent and the closest of friendships developed, which lasted and will continue to last. They are a warm and lively couple who always show genuine interest in what is happening to others and along with this comes understanding and a capacity to share. Over many years they had shared our joy and sadness and I shall never forget how supportive they were when we lost our daughter Anne for whom they had great affection.

They arrived about 11 o'clock with Sara and Matthew, their children, and we had a great day together. Norman, who is a highly qualified financial expert, is also a keen craftsman and has spent much of his leisure time exercising these skills. He had once doubled the size of his house in Hertfordshire, doing much of the work himself. This was a formidable project, but one completed with great success. He was just the man to examine what had been done at Overdale and to offer informed comment. Both Valerie and he were quite intrigued with the place for it was the sort of property they would have liked to own as a holiday retreat, although it was only a tenth of the size of their magnificent house in a village on the edge of Sheffield. Their opinion was that I had done exactly the right thing to come to the Cotswolds and they were certain the future was full of promise. Their visit gave me quite a boost for I valued their judgement, and to enjoy their company, if only for a short time, was a great joy.

I had seen little of Paul, the builder, since he had completed cleaning off and pointing the back of the house but he called in one day to discuss the possibility of cleaning off the roof tiles. It was not an essential job but he assured me that it would improve the look of the place and would not be a long job. The tiles, although asbestos, were a good imitation of Cotswold tiles and were widely used in the area. I conceded that an improvement in appearance for Overdale would be worthwhile and he set about the task with great enthusiasm. He continued to demonstrate the complete absence of fear that he had displayed in many of the other jobs he had done for me but this was the most hair-raising of all. He converted in Heath Robinson fashion a small ladder into a ridge ladder from which he intended to work, but in the event he spent more time off the ladder than on it, crawling about the roof with wire brush in hand, singing away contentedly as the moss and other accumulations yielded to the flourish of his brush. This was a virtuoso performance and in its way highly entertaining. It came as no surprise to me to learn, on one occasion when I visited him at home, that he had been awarded the highest commendation by his commanding officer when he was serving in the British Army of the Rhine. I spotted the commendation in a frame on the wall of his entrance hall, otherwise I would never have known. He had risked his life in the rescue of two German civilians who had got into difficulties when swimming in a deep water lake. When I raised this with him he brushed it off, saying it was no great feat. He claimed that anyone else could have done the same. I had my doubts about this contention having read the details of the rescue.

I was greatly relieved when he had completed the job, front and back, and gladly paid him for it. Sure enough, he was right. It took on the appearance of a new roof and, like a lady's new hat, added a special dimension to the overall appearance of Overdale.

The time had now come to give attention to the exterior decoration of the cottage, which meant doors and windows. Most were in fair order but one or two needed not only paint but also some minor repairs to the frames. I tackled the ones in most need of attention first, and as the weather was warm and dry the task was not at all unpleasant. Several sections of frame had to be chipped away and replaced with new pieces of timber, but once these were done, the job became quite straightforward. In many cases sanding was all that was necessary; in others some burning off was needed followed by replacement of putty. One or two of the frames were of steel, presumably replacements. There is no doubt that although not as aesthetically pleasing as timber frames, they scored highly in terms of durability and did not look too much out of place when painted white. There were five windows on the front and three on the gable end facing west, four at the back and two on the eastern gable end. I took a leisurely approach to the task and rang the changes by doing other things in between and so the days passed pleasantly by. The summer weather was now firmly established with sun from morning till night. On most days I took my ease at lunchtime in a deck chair on the lawn where I would have my sandwiches, bask in the peace and quiet of the place and get a healthy tan in the process. There were times when the quietness of it all and the warmth of the sun induced a period of sleep. Normally I would have scolded myself on the grounds that time in the day should be for work and not sleep. I took the very opposite view now and determined to take each day as it came and I achieved peak condition as a result. Lack of physical strength was certainly not going to stop me doing anything I wanted to do and I pushed myself to the limit in reclaiming the narrow piece of land across the road at the side of the house. I had given it the name of *The Jungle* for the undergrowth had become dense and the shrubs and trees had filled out so that just walking through this area was hard work. Fortunately I had some well developed skills in the use of hand tools, dating back to my days on the farm. Scythes, slashing hooks and billhooks, hedging hooks and fagging hooks were some of my favourite tools and, just as importantly, I could sharpen them all, a most critical skill with any cutting tool. When people find themselves unable to use such tools successfully, it is often because they are blunt and they are unable to put a cutting edge on them.

In tackling this task I knew that my main need would be stamina. The best way to deal with this was to approach the job gradually, adding a little extra each day after a gentle start. The undergrowth had to be cut, the level places by means of a scythe, the rough places with a fagging hook. Some of the shrubs had to be cut back and others cut down and dug out. Most of the sappling trees had to come out. My aim was to subjugate the growth to a point where I could operate freely with the Mountfield mower. From then on maintaining the piece in tidy fashion would be easy. The area had every appearance of having been a small orchard for at one end there were two apple trees of unknown quality; both were carrying a heavy crop of small apples which looked like developing. As autumn came there was a heavy crop but the quality was indifferent. As I worked away I toyed with the idea of developing the piece as an orchard but kept my options open. In due course it yielded to my determined and consistent effort and I was left with a mass of rough herbage, cuttings from trees and shrubs and uprooted saplings. As the weather was continuously dry my plan was to burn it all. In strategic points I established two substantial bonfires which smouldered away for days but eventually reduced everything to a pile of mainly wood ash. Another formidable project had been reduced to manageable proportions, and after spending a little time repairing one or two stretches of the stone walls surrounding the area, I left it and moved on to other matters.

At the bottom of this piece of land and opposite the front garden gate stood the old stable which had a mainly cobbled floor and was divided inside by a substantial partition to head height. In fact it was the orthodox standing for one horse and similar examples are still seen in the stable blocks of many of our country houses. Over a period, including my own contribution, this building had become a depository for a vast range of articles and material. Access to any of it was extremely difficult and I was forced into the position of doing something about it. The answer was to eliminate anything which was of no use and to stack the rest in a tidy fashion. Amongst the debris, by great good fortune, I found a number of stout plastic fertiliser bags which were ideal for accepting anything which I classified as rubbish and I soon had a number of these filled with a range of useless articles. One slight problem was the lack of light in the building. It was improved slightly when I pulled down the plastic bag substituting as window glass, and with the large door open I managed to complete the exercise, emerging as if from a deep coal mine, black all over. Order was now restored and room made for further incursion of materials and articles which I needed to store, or, more correctly, which I thought I needed to store. This syndrome is the story of my life and from which I never learn. Just occasionally some article stored for the day when I might require it, is picked up and used, but unfortunately the other 90 per cent takes up space which could be better used. But still, I never learn.

Apart from the entrance door the stable was well nigh invisible for it was buried in the most vigorous Russian Vine of all time. I swear it used to grow several inches each day and it was profuse. Even so it had merit and I was loath to remove it altogether. I compromised and cut it hard back but this only had the effect of making it grow stronger and faster. I was determined to eliminate it when the time was ripe.

I had cherished the hope that before too long I might get a visit from Michael and Inez Cropley and their boys, Timothy and Peter. As I said earlier they had shown me great kindness during and since my period of distress. Their house was always open to me and they invited me to meals on several occasions. I felt in some way or another I needed to show my appreciation for so much kindness. There was also another reason. Several years before, Michael and Inez had bought a derelict cottage in Eltisley and over time had transformed it into one of the prettiest places in the village. They are both highly talented people who make a success of everything they do but they are also perfectionists. In addition, over many years they have made a major contribution to the life of the village of Eltisley; Michael as vice-chairman of the Parish Council was the driving force behind the various tree planting schemes. His enthusiasm was infectious and several people put in an effort planting trees which have added to the beauty of the village landscape. This effort has significantly added to the heritage of the people of Eltisley. Inez as a member and office holder of the Women's Institute has used her many talents to good effect, and for the benefit of others.

When they rang and announced their visit I was more than pleased. Michael was an expert. He had performed a rare feat when he raised the derelict cottage in one piece some two feet off the ground and placed new foundations under it in order to increase the headroom inside the house. He had also added to the house in a highly professional way, ending up with a much enhanced dwelling and yet totally retaining the character of the original cottage. By comparison my efforts at Overdale were insignificant and I was a complete amateur alongside Michael. Nonetheless I knew they would be interested in what I was doing and should I need advice, it would be forthcoming.

They arrived on Saturday in time for lunch and were quite impressed with what they saw and were kind enough to say so. Overdale was a very different property from theirs and there were many things about it which had a strong appeal for them. The age and solidity of it stood out in their minds and the variety of features it contained took their eye. They seemed to like everything about it and congratulated me on what I had done. I valued their comments for they had gone through a similar experience with their own restoration although on a much larger scale.

After lunch we did a short tour of the Cotswolds but I wanted them to visit the Cotswold Countryside Collection at Northleach for I knew this would interest us all, but particularly the boys. The museum is on the site of the old prison at Northleach which in itself is worth a visit. We spent a long time looking at the fine collection of farm machinery and tools which have been assembled there and without a doubt the visit was a huge success with everyone. On Sunday morning we took a walk round the village, taking time to look in detail at some of the interesting buildings including the two churches and the Manor House. Because of work and school next day they moved off early after lunch and, as a parting gift, I presented them with a wrought iron firebasket of some vintage (at one time used in Overdale) as I knew they had been looking for one to put in the inglenook fireplace in their cottage. This gave them a great deal of pleasure as they knew its history and had seen where it used to be.

Their visit was one more on my list of those who I wished in some way to repay for their unstinting kindness. There were others who I still hoped would come. In the meantime I needed to take stock again of the progress I had made and decide what to do and in what order of priority I should proceed.

Chapter twelve

DESCENT INTO THE WELL

Considering the short time I had been at Overdale, several months of which had been winter, I had had quite a few visitors but with summer now in full flight the number increased. I believe my skills as host were improving and my visitors seemed to enjoy their stay. I had a telephone call from Douglas and Cynthia one Friday evening saying they were in Birmingham and would I be at home the next day. I had planned to go out at lunchtime but I deferred this and insisted they should come. They were friends of long standing dating back to the time when we all lived in Winchcombe. Their hospitality over many years had been generous and consistent. They had left Gloucestershire several years before, leaving a successful garage business behind, and bought a mushroom farm in Devon. In no time at all they transformed it into a profitable enterprise. They had considerable business acumen which they used to good effect but their success was also based on genuine hard work.

They arrived for coffee, accompanied by their daughter Paula who had made a great success of a career as an architect. They were very much Cotswold-orientated and thought that one day they might return to live there. We had a lightning tour of the cottage and the garden and it was very clear that they were much charmed by the place. As we had not met for quite some time there was much to talk about, but we kept coming back to the subject of Overdale. Paula of course had a special interest from an architect's point of view and asked a number of questions which demonstrated this. Time was short but they insisted in taking me out to the pub in the next hamlet for a very pleasant snack lunch. They dropped me back at Overdale and Douglas said that I had chosen well. He also indicated that if I ever thought of selling the place he might be interested. That seemed to me a very adequate endorsement that my decision to buy it had been wise.

This visit was quickly followed by an overnight stay by my brother Ron and his wife Mary on their way home from Bristol to Formby in Lancashire. I did my very best to make them welcome and comfortable and they were certainly very much at home during their short stay. Amongst other things we took a long walk into the country around the cottage and I explored this for the first time with them. Our journey had all the ingredients of a good country walk and it was warm and sunny. We walked away from Overdale up the hill, and on the edge of the village we joined a footpath which took us to the right across flat terrain. The Cotswold landscape rolled away from us on the left and we could hardly see any sign of habitation for miles. On our right, the upper reaches of the River Coln could be seen flowing gently through the centre of Shipton. The name of Shipton betrays the age of sheep farms and pens when the Abbot of Gloucester and the Bishop of Worcester kept large flocks of sheep in Shipton Oliffe and Shipton Solers. The footpath led us to a small wood through which we walked with some trepidation for there were notices saying 'private' at almost every turn. We did not walk into these areas but we were somewhat inhibited and began to think we must be on private land even though there was a well trodden path. Once outside the wood we turned back towards the village, keeping our fingers crossed that we would not bump into an irate landowner. We followed the stream to a point where it ran over the road. I had crossed this ford many times on my way out of the village in the car, thinking that one day, when time permitted, I would follow the stream up the valley. This was one of two fords in the village, the other being close by the church. We ambled through the village as far as Shipton Oliffe church and on a bit further to the tiny church of Shipton Solers. Although there were two villages they were treated as one and merged into one another. Put together they make only a tiny village and as individual entities are little more than hamlets. The contours of the place are very much up and down and this adds to the interest. There was no shop, no public house, but a substantial village hall stands on the corner of the village green which is well used by a number of organisations, the chief of which being the Women's Institute. This was a very active branch and organised open events in addition to their monthly meeting. These were well attended by the people of the village, and one of historical interest which I attended at Lorelei's invitation, was full to overflowing. From this experience it seemed to me that Shipton was a well integrated community. I had a certain amount of leg-pulling from Austin who in his own inimitable way insisted on casting me in the role of the eligible bachelor attending the Women's Institute. I found this amusing and was not offended but gratified to know that our relationship was such that Austin could do this without any inhibitions.

We turned back at the church and wended our way to Overdale where I had made provision for a wholesome snack lunch. They are both vegetarians and I had taken full account of this in my preparations. They both said how enjoyable it was. In the early afternoon they departed for Lancashire insisting that I had made them most comfortable overnight and expressing pleasure at seeing me settled so well at Overdale. They had shown great concern for my welfare over the past 12 months.

Towards the end of June I took off for Eltisley where Brenda had promised to put me up. The purpose of my visit was to attend a cricket match at Northampton where Yorkshire were the visitors. This had become an annual event for me and it all started a few years earlier when I was there in the spring watching Yorkshire and Northamptonshire. It was a cold and stormy day and I sat out in the open until a heavy shower developed, forcing me to seek shelter in a small covered stand. There was one other person in there and as we sat and ate our sandwiches, we talked. He was a very knowledgeable person about many things, especially cricket, and was a vice-president of the Northamptonshire cricket club. Above all he was a dedicated fan of Geoffrey Boycott. As we sat and talked I slowly came to the realisation that I should not have been sitting in that stand as it was reserved for vice presidents only. He dismissed my apologies saying that as a vice president he could invite a guest to join him at most matches to sit in the members' stand and I should consider that he had done just that. As play came to an end for the day he gave me a warm welcome to join him the next day and not only that, he would meet me at the turnstile where in his company I could go through at a reduced rate. I was highly honoured by such treatment. Our friendship has continued and although our meetings at the ground no longer take place, we still exchange greetings at Christmas. I will always remember Arnold's great kindness to me on so many occasions.

I invited Brenda to accompany me to the match and although she was slightly tempted to accept she had second thoughts as she had a number of things to do. I met Arnold and we had a good day's cricket and I accepted his invitation to meet him again on the Monday.

Brenda's hospitality was as usual most enjoyable and the weekend was full of interest in addition to the cricket but I came to the conclusion that I

The well

should not encroach further on her time. She had a very full programme in addition to her work and it was no small task for her to set aside time to accommodate me at the weekends. She had a living to earn and her two daughters to care for in addition to many friendships to pursue. She gave no hint of any reluctance for me to visit but made it very plain that I was welcome at any time. I felt however that I had to make a decision in my own mind to reduce the number of visits I made. I left Eltisley on Monday morning for Northampton having decided to return direct to Overdale when play ended that day. I took my leave of Arnold at the ground and drove through the Midlands to Overdale. As I travelled my thoughts were somewhat on the sombre side for I knew that I had made a decision which I always hoped I would never have to make. As I drove into the village my mood lifted for here I felt I had made my home and the prospects ahead were bright.

I had had one or two visits from Paul but there was some slight lull in activity, partly because I needed to use my capital sparingly at this stage. He had a burning desire to open up the well in the back garden. He had visions of this being made into a feature of the property and despite my reluctance to spend money on it he continued to raise the idea. I knew it was a very low priority and should have been rejected but in the end I gave in. Perhaps it might be a good proposition after all. The trade in bottled water was expanding rapidly and the water from this well might be saleable. I gave him clearance to start, on condition that we should proceed with caution particularly on the cash front. He threw himself into the project – not literally – with great enthusiasm and things began to hum. I had now been in residence for several months, but I had completely ignored the area of the top of the well. It was somewhat overgrown and topped by a wooden structure in the style of a dog kennel. Removing this was easy and revealed a rather rickety flat wooden cover on top of a wooden frame lying across the gap. It also revealed a neat little electric motor. All of this was easily removed and then we saw the well in all its glory. A long way below we could just see a glint of water as it reflected the light from the sky above us. We could also see clearly the first ten feet of dry walling which formed the lining of the well. We could hardly wait to fix up a long lead to a plug in the kitchen and to this we attached an inspection lamp of 150 watts. This was lowered slowly down the well enabling us to inspect the walls in detail as it went. It was quite a revelation for here was an outstanding piece of craftsmanship, a truly professional job. It was cylindrical in shape with a diameter of six feet and was approximately forty feet deep. The circular walls at the top were constructed of Cotswold stone and as the shaft descended it passed through strata of limestone rock. On one side a specially designed ladder was fixed to the wall and this also served as a frame to which the essential pipework was fixed which led to the pump at the bottom. The pump was worked by means of a shaft which was fixed to the cam, driven by the electric motor. On the face of it, it appeared that all the necessary equipment and pipes were in place to raise water from the well.

All of this filled us with excitement. We were like a couple of children with a new toy, but what appealed to us both was the standard of skill and craftsmanship which had given rise to this construction. It was a highly sophisticated water system which at one time brought an ample supply to the house, and on tap. It must have been one of the best systems in Shipton. Word went quickly round the village that the Overdale well had been opened and we had a constant stream of visitors asking if they might have a look at it. It was a minor sensation and as a result we learned quite a bit about it from local people who had known about it or heard from others. We learned that when it was in use before mains water came to the village it had never been known to run dry even in times of drought. Water from this well had been used by other households in the village when their own supply dried up. It also had the reputation of providing water of a very high quality.

All this stimulated our enthusiasm to proceed further and I quickly forgot the financial restraints associated with the project. At the end of that day we carefully covered the top, conscious that we now had a real hazard on our hands with a forty-foot drop into the abyss.

The following day was inspection day and we assembled quite early after breakfast. Paul had brought along his assistant for he felt that there could be risks involved in the next stage if there were only two participants. He also brought a long and very strong nylon rope which had all the appearance of an alpine climbing rope. By great good fortune there was an old cast iron, wooden-rollered mangle, very rusty, which stood in the area at the top of the well and it became clear that this was no coincidence. It was our belief that before the pump was introduced it would have been used as a hoist for a bucket used to lift water from the bottom. Paul worked away at this with his assistant with oil and spanner preparing it once again as a hoist. The rope was wound round the wooden roller. The handle on the roller was ratcheted and this provided a certain measure of control. Thus began Operation Descent, Paul volunteering to be the guinea pig. His intention was to descend the ladder with the rope tied round his middle so that if the ladder was rotten he would not drop to the bottom in free fall. He began to descend, issuing instructions as he went to me and his assistant at the top manning the mangle. Slowly and surely we lowered him and he made an examination as he went. In due course he arrived at the bottom and relayed to us a vivid description of what he saw. Apart from an easily removable small collection of debris he indicated that it was a fine sight to behold. There was about two feet of water and he could see the bottom as the water was crystal clear, and, he said, 'very cool'. He thought from a very cursory examination that the pump was in need of repair but that the ladder and framework were fairly sound. The most important thing of all was that he found the walls of the well to be in an excellent state. There was absolutely no sign of any of it breaking away. He seemed to be enjoying himself down there and still speaking with admiration about the craftsmanship. He announced his readiness to ascend and we took the strain on the lifting gear and started to wind. He arrived at the top and climbed out and immediately expressed the opinion that we should also go down and have a look. His assistant was the next man down and in due course he arrived back at the top and I steeled myself for the descent. I figured that as the system had been strong and efficient enough to lower and lift both of them, it would serve me well. I also had a great deal of trust in Paul's judgement. I knew he would not expose anyone to unnecessary risk. The descent was a new experience and the further one went, the more questions arose in one's mind. Suppose the walls fell in for some reason or the rope broke. Slowly the initial fears lifted and I began to enjoy the experience. The bottom of the well was wider than the rest and there was a lot of room to move about. It all seemed very secure down there and there seemed no chance at all of rock fall. The makers had done the job well. As Paul had reported, the water was very clear and very cool to the touch. It was obviously flowing very slowly across the bottom of the well. Looking upwards it seemed a long way to the top and the exit appeared to be quite small. One felt to be in a completely different world and having taken in my fill of the atmosphere, I decided it would be right to return to the top and I signalled my intentions. Slowly and surely I was hauled back up, glad to see the light of day. Paul expressed his satisfaction that the boss had been down the well.

I was now convinced that we ought to follow the inspection through, restore the system and get the water flowing. I could now leave it in Paul's hands and after further examination it transpired that the pump required reconditioning whereas the electric motor was in full working order. The work was spread over several weeks as Paul had other work on hand. This was fine by me as there was much to occupy me and no hurry.

I now tried my hand at wall building and pavement renovation. A short stretch of wall by the back garden gate was giving notice of collapse, some of the stones having already fallen out, and it generally looked untidy. I knew I ought to develop some skills in this craft as there must have been a total of some 100 yards of stone walls around and about the property and there were many places where some renovation was needed. On the face of it the task should not be beyond me and all the materials were to hand where gaps were appearing. The basic principle seems to be to build both sides of the wall with large stones and to fill the centre with small ones as you go. The larger ones should be at the bottom, getting smaller as one nears the top. There are a number of ways of putting the final course on the wall but the most common is to select longer stones which will straddle the wall and stand them on their side. Putting these principles into practice is hard and the key point is one of selection. Finding the right stone for the right place must come as a result of constant practice. Repairing a wall is of course easier than starting from scratch for all the materials are there and will not have moved far. I first of all moved all the stones which had fallen out of the wall away from the foot of the wall on each side, leaving room so that I could work close to it unhindered by stones under my feet. The act of doing this gave me a good opportunity to review the material I would be using. It was all a slow and somewhat painful process and like many other jobs there was an element of stress, for not only had the wall to look right, it also had to stand upright. Overriding everything else, it had to be safe and it must not fall down. Like many such things there was no single test which could be used to check its safety; perhaps this came with experience. I put the last stone on top of the wall and stood back as I had done frequently as work proceeded but I was not pleased with my handiwork. I could not even say I was satisfied for it stood out like a sore thumb when compared with the rest of the wall. The best I could say was that it seemed to be safe and for the rest I could only hope that the stones would weather and look more like a wall than just a heap of stones. The next time I tried my hand at this craft was on the walls surrounding the long narrow piece, the former orchard. It all became a little easier although there was still much trial and error involved. I believe the real craftsmen say, 'Never handle the same stone twice'. I was miles away from achieving such perfection and at no point did I feel satisfied. Almost every day as I moved about the property the walls served to taunt me, crying out for the skilled hands of an expert.

I then moved on to the paved areas at the back and down the side of the cottage. The whole of this was in poor shape and the only solution was to go systematically round and where necessary re-lay all the offending stones. Starting at the steps at the back I adjusted the stones to a uniform level, taking the top of the steps as a baseline. They were of course Cotswold stones and all of irregular shapes so the style was of crazy paving. Using sand as a foundation I made good progress and found it much easier than rebuilding walls and distinctly more satisfying. After laying the first few stones I made a mortar mix and fixed them in place and could now proceed with confidence using a spirit level to check as I went along. There had to be a slight fall on the pathway to avoid the water collecting in embarrassing puddles when it rained. The job went well along the back of the cottage and kept me busy for a few days. It became more complicated when I came to the steps under the gable end. There was only a trace of steps, but, using the pattern, I managed to produce a range of steps along the full length of the gable end, again secured with mortar. I fixed the last step and felt far more satisfied with my efforts than with the wall building.

There was further activity at the well. Paul had taken the pump to an expert in Cheltenham for repairs and had been advised that it was ready for collection. On his return he showed it to me with great pride. It was quite a showpiece, some three feet long and now gleaming as it was made of solid brass. It was lowered into the bottom of the well with great care, to Paul who had climbed down the ladder, now made safe. After a day's work he announced that tomorrow would be well opening day and expressed a wish that *the boss* should be there to witness the event. I happily fell in with the plan for I was just as excited at the prospect of water flowing from the well as he was. On the following morning only one job remained. This was the connecting of the shaft which activated the pump to the electric motor at the top. The critical factor was one of alignment but after a struggle a dummy run was made, activating the plunger on the pump by hand. All seemed well and the motor was switched on. Much to my surprise, water gushed out of the pipe running to the top of the well and continued to flow as long as the motor operated. There seemed to be no point in letting the motor run indefinitely and it was switched off. We now had a well with an unending supply of water which could be made to flow at the flick of a switch, but to what end? Unless we had an acute drought or the mains supply became contaminated we would be hard-pressed to justify using it. It might become known as Hardy's folly and perhaps in a way it was. The adventure had cost me over £250 and I found such expenditure hard to justify.

On one of their visits Paul and Anne presented me with a small electric pump for use in the pond, a most ingenious device driven by electricity and yet which could be submerged in the pond. It was designed to do two things: to lift water from the pond to a higher level and to provide a fountain. After clearing the weeds from the rocks, down which the water would flow back into the pond, we set it up and got it to work. It did everything which was claimed of it and when in operation the trickle of the water down the rock face and the operation of the fountain brought this corner of the garden to life. It was pleasant to hear the flow of water on a hot afternoon and it provided an added dimension to the fast improving garden.

The summer was turning out to be near perfect. July was hot and sunny and I spent much of the time out of doors maintaining the gardens and grounds and week by week finding odd jobs, all of which made for a general improvement in the appearance of the outside and the inside of Overdale. As we moved into August I felt that all sense of urgency to get things done had now passed. I had plenty of time to do just exactly as I wished and I ceased to make any ambitious plans. I was occasionally stung into action by Paul and on one occasion he announced that we ought to renovate the roof of the kitchen. It was impossible to resist this advice for it was the one part of the building which had not been touched and now stood out like a sore thumb. It was obvious from looking at the contours of the roof that the battens holding the Welsh slate tiles were rotten, and some of the tiles needed replacing. I asked him to take on the job and he immediately set to work taking off the tiles. I have never met anyone before or since who tackled any job with such enthusiasm. Whilst most of us think long and hard before we embark on a job, he would start immediately and in no time at all, something big was happening and often it was a bit of a shock to the system. This was no exception and it surprised me to see how easily the tiles came off in his expert hands. In no time they were all neatly stacked ready for re-use. Unfortunately just as he had finished it started to rain, this after a very long dry spell, and worse, it was the end of the week. He dashed off and returned with a huge piece of thick polythene sheet with which he briskly covered over the bare battens. On Monday he returned with new lengths of battening and after ripping off the old he began to fit the new. By early afternoon he was re-laying the tiles. The speed of the operation was beyond belief. There was a slight delay in progress when he had to go and find tiles to replace those which were already cracked or which cracked when being taken off. I was intrigued by the new tiles which had a feel of rubber about them. They were in fact plastic, with an almost indefinite length of life and apparently almost unbreakable. Most importantly they were only marginally more expensive than Welsh slate. A new piece of guttering and fascia board were fixed, the flashing onto the house wall put in place and another major job was completed. This was about the last of the eyesores dealt with and in such an expeditious manner. I felt grateful to Paul for selling the idea to me.

The rest of August was enjoyable but uneventful. It was time for entertaining and I had a visit from Cynthia and Roy who still believed I was mad to stay at Overdale. They did, however, acknowledge how much the place had been improved since their last visit and how clean and comfortable it was compared with those early spartan days of February. Their view was that I ought to get out before the winter came. It was no place for a bachelor. They were genuinely concerned for my welfare but did not appreciate how attached I had become to the cottage and its environment.

Harry was a frequent visitor and would pick me up at about 7.30 pm and drive to a pub in Andoversford for a couple of drinks. I used to look forward to these weekly visits for we had much in common, in particular all the happy days we had spent together when Doris was alive.

Paul and Anne were on their summer vacation from teaching and came on one or two Saturday evenings for a meal. We would take our drinks on the lawn at the back, with me dashing up and down the steps to the kitchen to keep an eye on the cooking. I had now had sufficient practice to produce an acceptable meal without panic and I got a lot of pleasure from their visits, and I believed they felt the same.

In this relaxed frame of mind I decided to take a holiday and I had a very strong desire for a period of solitude. My conviction was that the best place to find this atmosphere would be in an isolated cottage somewhere on the west coast of Scotland. I spotted an advertisement in the Guardian stating that a large selection of cottages was available and would be found in their brochure. A telephone call led to the arrival of the brochure by post. I had spent two lovely holidays in Scotland with Doris and we came to know it well, particularly the west coast. I selected a cottage on the southern shore of Loch Ewe at Inverasdale which had views up the loch to Inverewe with its famous gardens and across to Aultbea on the northern shore. Seeing the name of Aultbea brought back happy memories for we once spent a most enjoyable night there. I also remember walking along the road skirting the loch on my own before our evening meal, and hearing a voice shouting for help. I rushed in the direction of the cries to find that it was the local doctor calling on me for assistance. When I got to him he asked me to help carry an elderly lady into his surgery. It transpired that he had been called out to a road accident and had brought two casualties back to his surgery for first aid treatment. One of the two ladies was immobile with a suspected fracture of the ankle. Having helped him to carry the lady into the surgery, I expressed a wish to stay and help further but he said there was nothing I could do and he was summoning an ambulance to take both ladies to the hospital at Inverness some 60 miles away. This incident underlined for me the remoteness of the communities in that part of Scotland. It also illustrated the difficulties faced by doctors in providing help to the people living there.

All of this persuaded me that the chosen cottage was the right one and I booked it for early October. I could now prepare for the event which was to turn my world on its head and the ramifications of which were considerable.

Chapter thirteen

ESCAPE TO SCOTLAND

The one person who had not yet been able to visit Overdale was Pam, mainly because of her work commitments. Soon after early retirement at 51, Pam had been invited to take a part-time post as Supervisor of Agricultural Apprentices and new entrants in Suffolk, by the Agricultural Training Board and she had become very much involved in this work. Her job was top priority in her mind and she saw it as a real commitment to the young men and women involved and to their employers and was somewhat reluctant to leave the job for any length of time. At last she promised to come to Overdale for a few days, and the date fixed was 12th September. I looked forward very much to her visit, although with a certain amount of nervousness. Could I provide her with a good holiday, could I make her stay a comfortable one, and how should we occupy our time? These were all questions which did not arise when I had been preparing to receive married couples or families. Married people have each other's company and in addition, perhaps, their children. To this extent they are sharing the experience together and the host need not get too involved. In the case of a single guest the host must be more closely involved if the person is not to feel lonely in a new environment. I knew Pam would make herself at home and was easy company and yet I felt extremely nervous. I have since often tried to analyse these feelings but not with any success.

I did a thorough cleaning and polishing and laid in a good variety of food. In a way this contributed to my nervousness for Pam was such an excellent cook and I knew my food would not be more than average. The journey from Glemsford to Overdale is extremely complex for it is very much across country and follows none of the main arterial routes. I tried to make it easier by sending a clear and simple route map of my own design (picking out landmarks) which could be read at intervals and hopefully understood. We had spoken on the telephone about approximate arrival time, and Pam, true to form, arrived within a few minutes of it. I am afraid my greeting was very formal but I was genuinely pleased that she had made such an effort and done me the honour of coming to Overdale. It was now up to me to make her journey worthwhile.

There was much to talk about and much to show her in the house and in the garden but there was plenty of time. The first essential was that she should rest and relax after her journey. I took her bag and showed her to her room, the main bedroom, leaving her to her own devices whilst I made a cup of coffee and made a start on the preparations for the evening meal. When she came down and after the coffee we did a tour of the house and had an initial look at the garden. Then it was gin and tonics and second gin and tonics before we sat down to a leisurely meal. We talked over our coffee for some long time and then after a joint effort at washing up Pam retired to bed. She warned me that she would be likely to be reading until well into the night. She is an avid reader and the book at bedtime is an essential part of her life.

I retired some time later and for some reason found sleep not too easy. I think I was occupied thinking out plans for how we might spend the next day. After a full English breakfast, we set off in my car and I looked forward to an enjoyable day in Pam's company. We spent a few hours in Cheltenham where I took the opportunity of doing my weekly shopping and showed Pam some of Cheltenham's well-known sights, such as the Pitville Gardens and the Promenade. The Promenade was always thought to be something special with its Cavendish House and other up-market shops, and it still retains something of that aura although some dilution was taking place as a result of some of the premises being taken over by the national chains.

We left Cheltenham and climbed over Cleeve Hill to Winchcombe, stopping at the top to take in the view of the Severn Valley and beyond. Winchcombe was the right place to stop for a snack lunch and we enjoyed the atmosphere of the flagstoned, inglenooked bar of the once famous George Hotel. It was a place I knew well from the days when we lived at the Home Farm at Sudeley Castle. After lunch we strolled round the little town and then on the road again along the lanes which ran through the land which made up the Home Farm and out onto the Broadway road. We made a detour through Stanton and Stanway and then parked the car in Broadway. It was full of cars and people with whom we mingled in the almost compulsory stroll up and down the main street. Broadway is a pretty sight in the early morning before the cars begin to gather, but by 10.30 am it lies buried in cars and people, and loses much of its genuine charm. This is not something to complain about, for people do want to see these places and their fame cannot be denied. We climbed out of Broadway on the road to Snowshill and then wended our way slowly back to Overdale. It had been a good day and I had enjoyed Pam's company as my companion for the day, feeling rather proud of the fact that she had chosen to come to the Cotswolds and spend time with me. I was beginning to relax in her company.

We had made a brief stop on our journey that day at a garden centre just outside Winchcombe and Pam bought me two container rose bushes. They carried blooms and she insisted that I made my own selection. The choice was very wide but two stood out for me, Bettina and Lilian Wheatcroft. I unloaded them when we got home and made a decision about where each should go.

I cannot remember the menu I had planned for that evening but I do remember that I had quite a lot of help from Pam in the kitchen. It was a delight to have her company in such a domestic situation and time passed too quickly.

Friday came and the weather continued to favour us. Having travelled north on Thursday, I felt that Pam would enjoy the contrasting scenery of the south Cotswolds. Our journey took us through the delightful valley of the River Coln, through Compton Abdale, Coln St Denis and on to Bibury where we walked along the river, amply stocked with trout, round to the water mill and across the meadow to the famous Arlington Row and back to the car. On then to Coln St Aldwyn and up to this point, we had been following the course of the River Coln which had its beginnings in the village of Shipton. It had now become a river of some size, making its way to Lechdale where it joins the River Thames. It was interesting to think that the tiny stream which I could see out of the front window of Overdale in the small village of Shipton Oliffe, ultimately found its way to the sea through the great City of London.

Leaving Coln St Aldwyn we turned west to Ampney Crucis and then to the great Cotswold wool town of Cirencester with its magnificent church, known as the Cathedral of the Cotswolds. After a nose round some of the shops we took the Stroud road, skirting the famous Bathurst Park estate and on to Minchinhampton Common where we stopped at a small pub for a lunchtime snack. Our ultimate destination was Chalford at the head of the Stroud valley, a village of some importance and size, and built on a steep hillside. Chalford rises some 400 feet from the valley floor where there are still traces of the woollen cloth industry mills which were spread through the valley to Stroud. The village is large by Cotswold standards but I imagine it is prettier now than it has ever been and unspoiled by any traces of industry. It is a light and airy place but not one suited to those who are less agile or of unsound heart. The views from the top across the village are full of interest. Many of the mostly small houses would have been occupied by those who laboured in the mills and who at the end of the day had to make their way home up the most challenging of slopes. Despite all this there are still many people who choose to find a home in Chalford and properties are snapped up. The streets are narrow and not given to too much traffic. Some of the houses cannot be reached by car and the last several yards have to be covered on foot. It is clearly a place where people go to live who want to live at Chalford for what it is. I imagine this makes for a unique community and it is certainly a village not to be missed by those who wish to know the Cotswolds. I shall always remember my visit there in Pam's company.

We took the most direct route home for I had booked a table at the Red Lion in Northleach for our evening meal, a most enjoyable event, and the food, although not exciting, was a good deal better than anything I could produce. The evening out was the climax of an outstandingly enjoyable day, and there were more to come.

On Saturday we had decided to stay at home and Pam insisted that she would give me a hand in the garden and also prepare an evening meal. It was very clear to me now that we both felt very easy in each other's company and as far as I was concerned I wanted this to go on although I was well aware that within a day or two she would be returning home. I tried to shut this out of my mind. We spent a leisurely day with Pam weeding one or two of the borders and I took the opportunity to mow the grass.

Sunday was a very full day. I had been invited to a family garden party by Cynthia and Roy to celebrate the christening of one of Roy's grandchildren. When I had the call about this from Cynthia I said I would have a guest staying for a few days and it would not be possible to attend. This provoked a sharp retort from Cynthia who insisted that my visitor would be most welcome as a guest at the party. She was obviously quite intrigued when I explained about Pam and was eager to meet her. Harry paid us a visit in the morning as he often did on a Sunday and was in his most entertaining mood. There was much laughter and no shortage of leg-pulling, mainly at my expense. There are people who can be quite offensive when

The renovated kitchen

following these tactics, but Harry never gave offence. It was all good fun and he could also be very serious-minded. His experience had been wide and varied, from driving goods and passenger trains into Paddington at the height of the Blitz (about which he has a store of memories which make fascinating listening) to the years he spent driving huge diesel locomotives of the East African Railways in Kenya. I never tire of him recounting these stories for he has the knack of sustaining the suspense for long periods. He is a very effective natural storyteller.

In the afternoon we joined the party which was being held in Cynthia and Roy's spacious and immaculate garden. This was some event, complete with small marquee and the weather was quite special. It allowed everyone the rare opportunity to wear their very best summery clothes and a charming sight it made. Pam and I were given a very warm welcome and altogether it was a most enjoyable event. What stood out for me was the special welcome which Cynthia and Roy gave to Pam. It was a busy time for them with family and friends in large numbers but they took time to make Pam feel very much at home and like one of the family.

We had to leave early and get back to Overdale in time to prepare for a visit to Paul and Anne for an evening meal. The invitation had pleased me greatly for I was keen that they should meet Pam. The meal was excellent, the conversation lively and it was enjoyed by us all. I had no doubts about the success of the evening for it was a most relaxed affair with good food and wine and a good relationship was built between Pam and Paul and Anne.

Stratford-upon-Avon was our destination on the following day and this was full of interest. Although I was not unfamiliar with the place I had never *done the tour.* We explored together, first Anne Hathaway's Cottage which totally absorbed us, so much so that two separate American parties went through the place in quick succession leaving us absolutely standing. They could say that they had 'seen it', but we could say that we had explored it pretty fully. (To be fair, we undoubtedly had more time to give to the visit.) From there we walked to the town centre with its collection of attractive buildings and more particularly the birthplace of William Shakespeare. This has a fine story to tell and an atmosphere of Tudor times to flavour the story. We strolled down to the river and the precincts of the Memorial Theatre at lunchtime and took our lunch in the famous Swan's Nest. Very much a day to remember. Although I had known Pam a very long time I felt now that we had come closer together during her visit and that I was going to miss her badly when the time for her departure came. I had no idea as to how she felt about me and I had no reason to believe that there had been any change in our established relationship covering a number of years.

On Tuesday we took a leisurely ride to Winchcombe and then on to Tewkesbury, another town full of medieval buildings and with a magnificent Cathedral in which we spent much of our time. We took afternoon tea down by the River Avon at the Water Mill and then made our way home.

After our evening meal we sat and talked seriously about our feelings and beliefs, and our general philosophy of life. We spoke in particular about how our experiences had brought us to the views we held and the feelings we were subjected to. It became clear to me that Pam, having lived on her own for many years after a long marriage, had met and conquered the challenges which arise from such a situation and had no intention of changing this. She had played a major part in bringing up three children and had worked very hard in doing so. They were all now well established and Pam felt totally free to do as she wished with no family responsibilities which need concern her. She owned her own house and car and was able to live just as she pleased. She had long ago determined that she would not marry again. I felt that this was a very carefully thought-out decision and one which was unlikely to be reversed. I ought not to have been disappointed to hear this but I have to confess that I was, for my feelings at this point, heightened by the great time we had spent together, were that I would wish to explore our relationship further. Such was my arrogance in thinking she might want to do the same that I felt rebuffed when she told me of her own intentions for the future. No more was said that night nor the next morning when Pam had to leave Overdale and return home. I had to content myself with the feeling that she had enjoyed her stay and I am sure she had enjoyed my company as I had most certainly enjoyed hers. We said our goodbyes and Pam departed but the next few hours were full of torment. I felt desperately lonely and wished she had not had to go. For a short time I had been living on a high and now I was really on the floor. I telephoned her the next day and the day after that and that gave me some consolation. She was aware that I was going to Scotland for I had tried to persuade her to come with me but her commitments made such a proposal out of the question. She did however say that she hoped we would keep in touch.

Paul, the builder, had visited me once or twice during the period to tidy up a few loose ends prior to starting a major operation on the gable end at the western end of the house and had been at his most polite to Pam, although not without showing a touch of his sharp wit, the subject of which was *the boss*. He came along on the day of Pam's departure to discuss the work ahead but could not resist sounding me out on how Pam fitted into the picture. He was absolutely certain that I must invite her again and spoke in glowing terms about her. She had obviously made a big hit with him. I was quite non-committal in my response to all of this, but I know he was concerned for my welfare and, in his mind, seeing more of Pam would be a great thing for me.

As I would be leaving for Scotland within a week, there were a number of matters to arrange. Paul had a policy about the house which I needed to go along with and that was that he did not want to hold a key. I could see his point and asked my neighbours Fred and Hilary Bate if they would mind holding the keys in my absence. I had suggested to Paul that if for any reason he had to get into the house he could borrow the key and return it and this he quite accepted. Fred and Hilary had become firm friends, always willing and anxious to offer help, and I occasionally sought their advice.

The project at the gable end was to clean and point the stonework and this was likely to occupy Paul for most of the time whilst I was away as he would not be working full time on it. He made a start and was working from the top downwards on the cleaning process when he discovered a major problem. He found that the lintel above the window of the bedroom was cracked in two places and would have to be replaced. It could not be left as it was bearing an enormous weight of stone and could have collapsed at any time. I had no hesitation in agreeing that it should be replaced as the risks in leaving it were frightening. The window was above the road used frequently by people out walking and so the sooner it was done the better.

Paul went in search of a lintel and returned in a few hours with a re-inforced concrete lintel on the back seat of his car. It was very heavy and by no means easy for Paul and his assistant, who had been drafted in, to extract it from the car. It certainly did no good at all to the back seat and interior of the car. There was only one day left before my departure and the last decision I had to make was to agree that scaffolding should be hired for the purpose of replacing the cracked lintel with the new one. Again I quickly agreed to this for there was no alternative. In the event the cost was kept to a minimum by Paul arranging to have it for the shortest possible time. The account totalled £46 and Paul worked in perfect safety.

On Tuesday morning, 25th September, I left Overdale on my long journey to Scotland and took my leave of Paul who was at work on the gable end. The job was in its initial stages but I could see that there would be a transformation by the time I returned and this cheered me on my way.

The first leg of the trip took me as far as Morecambe on the Lancashire coast. I had often promised myself that I would look up an old friend and his wife who had been there for many years and I rang them from a point on the A6. They urged me to call and asked me if I could stay the night. This was not my intention but I gladly accepted their generous hospitality. I was quite overwhelmed by their warm welcome and there was much to talk about. They knew of the recent happenings in my life and we talked about old times. I learned that they continued to live a very full and active life, much of it in pursuit of the welfare of others, particularly amongst young people. I left the next morning having dug at the deep well of nostalgia which our meeting stimulated.

On now over Shap and into the clouds on the A6 to Penrith where I bought a couple of pork pies to keep me going until my evening meal. I crossed the Scottish border and took the M9 to Stirling and then on to the A82 to Loch Earn and Lochearnhead where I spotted a neat and clean looking guest house. I parked up and to my delight found that they could accommodate me for the night. The married couple who ran the place were involved in the air traffic business, he in air traffic control and she as an air hostess. It seemed that they worked different shifts and it was not difficult to run the guest house business with such an arrangement. It appeared to work well for their standards were quite high. Their aim was to retire soon and run the guest house full time. I made an early start, intent now on seeing again some of the places we had visited before and I still had one more night before I could take over the cottage. One tends to forget distances when looking at a road map of Scotland but time was not important at this stage. I followed the A82, crossing the bridge at Ballachulish (I remember crossing the loch here on the famous ferry before the bridge was built) and then took the Corran ferry across Loch Linnhe and south to the head of Loch Sunart. This took me into the centre of the three areas I wished to see again, namely Morvern, Ardnamurchan and Moidart. The landscapes in Scotland are always compelling, often dramatic and sometimes breathtaking, but it is the infinite variety of the scenery which makes Scotland one of the most beautiful places in the world. Round every corner, over each hill and across the mountain ranges in which are set the fresh and seawater lochs, the scenery is quite beyond comparison. The particular area I wanted to see again had many of these qualities but its special appeal was its remoteness and its tranquillity. I arrived at the head of the loch in the tiny village of Strontian with its gathering of little white local authority houses set on the edge of the loch. The only other building of any consequence was the hotel where I booked a room and evening meal. Having freshened up I took the welcome opportunity of a stroll along the side of the loch, free from the persistent noise of the car engine which had been with me all day. I was struck again by the silence and tranquillity of the place, the silence broken only by the noise coming from a small boat moving gently across the loch on its way home from a day's fishing. I found it difficult to believe that anyone lived here for there were no signs or sounds of people. I turned round after about a mile and returned to the hotel for what turned out to be a splendid meal in a dining room of victorian vintage and of great appeal to me. Nothing had been changed over many years but it had been kept fresh by expert interior decorators. I telephoned Pam after dinner and described my resting place for the night. She was obviously pleased to hear from me again and I began to feel that she was not just being polite. I went to bed feeling elated and pleasantly tired. As I read for a while (I managed to secure a *Guardian* that day) I found the noise from the hotel bar somewhat disturbing. It was the noise of a juke box and laughter but I consoled myself by thinking that by 11 o'clock or so when they all went home, silence would reign. I slept for a short time but wakened to the noise of chattering and loud laughter. The music had stopped and I imagined they were all taking their leave. An hour later I awoke again and found it hard to believe that it was 1 o'clock in the morning and the noise below was even worse. My sleep was sporadic and I did not settle until 3 o'clock when suddenly everything went quiet. When I tentatively raised this with the landlady at breakfast and asked whether there had been some special celebration last night, she shrugged it off by saying that it did happen occasionally and apologised to me for the inconvenience caused. The irony to me was that in such a quiet and tranquil place by day, the night I spent there was the worst I had ever spent in any hotel anywhere. Over the years I had spent nights in many different places from London to Paris and in many parts of the UK. I hoped for the landlady's sake that it was a one-off event.

I could not take up residence in the cottage until mid-afternoon that day and I judged I could spend an hour or two looking again at the area alongside the loch. The point of Ardamurchan seemed to be an exciting objective as we had not gone so far west on our last trip. The road ran alongside the loch almost to the point, and dotted along it were small hamlets supporting a very small population. Apart from some fishing and a fairly primitive agriculture it was difficult to imagine how people survived. It was obviously a struggle. The point itself was devoid of people and almost uncultivated apart from small patches of grass enclosed by rickety stone walls. A few sheep and a handful of grazing cattle nibbled at the shortest of short grass but nothing else was to be seen except sea birds, all of which seemed surprised to see a human being amongst them. By 11 o'clock I needed to head in the direction of Gairloch if I was to arrive at about the agreed time. My route took me through Fort William and then on the A87 to the Kyle of Lochalsh, Achnasheen, Kinlochewe, Gairloch and finally to Poolewe. From the village it was a short run alongside the loch to Inverasdale, where following instructions from the owner, the cottage was easily found. It was all and more than I could wish for, commanding magnificent views across Loch Ewe, and the ground in front ran down to a clean sandy beach. One could look back up the loch to the heavily wooded area which surrounds the famous Inverewe gardens. It was an ideal place, off the beaten track and yet giving access to a wealth of ideal walking country. It was an original crofter's dwelling and was well preserved yet with all the conveniences of modern living, clean and well-equipped, with ample sources of heat and light. I knew I would be content there and settled down quickly. As there were three bedrooms, I had to make a decision on which to use. I chose the one with the most comfortable bed.

My plan for the holiday was to do as much walking as I could and in the event this was what I did, favoured by some excellent autumn weather and an almost complete absence of rain. I daily packed a snack lunch with an ample supply of hot water in a flask for tea making, loaded this into the car along with my rainwear, and away I went. The story which unfolded would be long in the telling for I packed much into the time and walked miles and miles, drinking in the magnificence and beauty of the countryside. I became so entranced by it all that I began to entertain the idea of moving to this part of Scotland to live out my life in peace and tranquillity. The idea came to the surface one afternoon as I walked round the shores of Loch Gairloch. It was warm and sunny and the water of the loch was blue. The small fishing vessels were anchored in the harbour surrounded by a handful of private yachts and all seemed magical and very tempting. As I walked I came across two or three dwellings with For Sale notices outside, and one in particular took my eye. It was a modern bungalow on top of a slope which led down to the edge of the loch and looked across to Gairloch harbour. My thoughts made me bold and I approached the front door of the property and rang the bell. A man of about 55 answered my call and I told him that I was interested in the property, did he have a copy of the details which I could study? He invited me in and sat me down and then brought the details. This was accompanied by an offer to show me over the property. It was as good inside as it was outside and most attractively equipped and decorated. It was in a very saleable condition and as far as I could see had no snags except perhaps its location. For many it would have been too far from shops and services but as far as I was concerned this would have been no disadvantage (at least at this stage in my life).

The above incident happened early on in my stay and my ideas and feelings then began to change dramatically. I had received one or two letters from Pam to which I had replied immediately and I followed this up with a telephone call each night. It was clear to me that something was happening between us although we were separated by some 600 miles. Day by day the feeling became more intense to the point where I could easily have packed up and left the cottage with no regrets. I knew on the other hand that it would be unfair to jump to conclusions about Pam's feelings. I knew how I felt but I must contain these feelings until I was certain that I was not deluding myself. I was now on another high and life seemed absolutely wonderful. The idea of moving to Scotland rapidly faded and I realised how stupid it was. Each night I drove along the road about a mile to the telephone box and telephoned Pam, until one night in the middle of trying to reach her the whole thing packed up. I could have smashed it to pieces in my bitter disappointment that I could not contact her. I had to abandon any further attempt that night and in future drove three miles to the next nearest box.

I now became slightly impatient to go home and see Pam again and I got the feeling that my presence would be welcomed, but at the same time I felt that I must stay and get the full benefit from the cottage and the place. On the Thursday before leaving on Friday I wanted to realise a wish I had held all through the holiday – to see a herd of deer in this most natural environment, and I determined to walk until I did. I followed the course of the stream which spilled into the loch at Poolewe for there was a good track and no notices indicating that it was private. I walked and climbed steadily for two hours with no sign of deer and eventually I got out on to the moor. In due course I came upon a tarn when the track ran out and I found myself in the middle of a bog. I had cherished the idea that the track would lead me ultimately on to another road, as the map seemed to indicate this, but this was clearly not the case and I had to turn round and retrace my steps. I now had a problem for within about an hour and a half the light would fade. I had to get back to landmarks before this happened and instead of walking I had to march at a brisk pace. My anxiety began to fade as I picked out in front of me some of the places I had noted on the way out and I now had bearings to work to. Dusk was approaching quickly and as I was descending from a hill I heard the electrifying call of a stag; as I looked across in the twilight I could see him moving stealthily across the slope followed by a handful of young deer some fifty yards away. It was a thrilling experience which I will always remember. This crowned my day and my holiday and when I got back to the cottage I cooked and enjoyed an enormous meal and then fell asleep in front of the fire. After a while I awoke and took myself off to bed for tomorrow I had to leave for Overdale, and, as soon as possible, visit Pam.

I broke my journey at Formby where I stayed overnight with my brother Ron and his wife Mary; they are both lovers of Scotland and there was no shortage of things to talk about. Years before they had spent two weeks in a cottage at Inverasdale not far from the one I had occupied, a very strange coincidence. Next morning, fortified with an excellent vegetarian breakfast, a novel change for me, I moved off on the last leg of my journey to the Cotswolds and Overdale, and I was eager to see it again.

Chapter fourteen

THE END OF THE AFFAIR

It was dark when I arrived back at Overdale so my inspection of Paul's work would have to wait until next morning. I telephoned Pam and brought her up to date with my news and at the same time tentatively raised the possibility of my spending a few days with her in Suffolk once I had got things in hand at Overdale. To my delight she was happy with this suggestion and I felt very good about the prospects before me. I cooked a meal and turned in early. The 550-mile journey from Inverasdale, although broken by an overnight stop, had been quite taxing and I slept soundly.

I woke as it was getting light and got up immediately. There was so much I wanted to do particularly as my aim was to leave for Suffolk as soon as possible. I contained my curiousity and had breakfast before going outside to check on what had been done. I knew that if I went out first my breakfast would be long delayed.

I was very impressed when I saw the transformation to the gable end. Paul had excelled himself for now one could see how attractive the Cotswold stone wall was when cleaned and neatly pointed. There was no pattern in the stonework of the cottage and this was part of its appeal. Paul's work had brought this to life and I was delighted. This had been his main task and I was glad that I had followed his suggestion and had it done, for as one approached the cottage across the green it now stood out and this was the first impression anyone would get of Overdale. Paul had accomplished a veritable miracle and with minimum disturbance. The only follow-up was a fairly major cleaning operation in the bedroom where the lintel replacement had taken place. The whole bedroom, bedcovers, carpets, curtains and furniture appeared to have suffered from a hurricane. There were grit, sand, stones and dust to be cleared and, where disturbance resulting from the construction work had occurred, the plaster had been broken away. The cleaning was top priority; this completed I turned my attention to other urgent matters such as mowing grass and cleaning up the borders which in my absence of nearly three weeks had flourished. After all the reclamation I had done, the mowing was about a day's task when trimming the edges and clipping areas inaccessible to the Mountfield were included. I never found this job irksome for, as with many jobs concerned with gardening, at the end of the day there was something to be seen for the effort. It all looked neat and tidy once more.

The following day was given over to the cleaning of the borders. Although autumn was upon us the weeds had flourished in my absence. The situation was more controllable now than it had been in early spring and most weeds pulled easily so I covered the ground quickly.

I did not see Paul for a day or two but when he came I expressed my thanks for the effort he had made in my absence and congratulated him on the excellent results. He was particularly pleased when I told him that I would be spending a few days with Pam in Suffolk. He could not stop talking about it and was genuinely pleased for me. I began to feel a bit concerned at this point because there was not much work that I could find for him to do. Most of what was left now I could do myself and in any case the money I had set aside for spending on Overdale was getting low. Paul always understood that such a time would come and when I raised it with him he accepted the position quite philosophically, saying that I should contact him if anything did crop up and he would gladly come. Fortunately he had one or two things lined up which would keep him occupied. Apart from everything else his presence about the place when I needed some support had been invaluable. I told him about this and he was pleased that he had been of such help. I know that he had been aware of my plight and had responded positively, a rare gift not possessed by many. I shall always be grateful for what he did.

I was moving now into uncharted waters and Overdale was beginning to move slightly from the front page. Pam had expressed her pleasure about my forthcoming visit and I was now preparing for my departure. The garden was in hand, the house was clean and tidy and I could now lock it up and forget it, giving my attention to more important matters.

On the morning of 23rd October I packed my bag, taking care to put in enough clothes to last me at least a week, handed the keys to Hilary and Fred saying that I was not certain of the exact date of my return, and set off for Glemsford in Suffolk. As I travelled I kept coming back to the question of how significant this journey might be. My feelings towards Pam had grown in the period between her visit and now into ones of considerable affection and I knew I must see her, but did she feel the same? Such emotions tormented me and I just had to find out. On arrival she gave me the most warm and affectionate welcome and I sensed immediately that our feelings were mutual.

We spent a joyous and emotionally highly-charged week together and found ourselves in the position of wanting it to continue. As we were both completely free agents we decided that nothing would stand in our way. We would get married at an early date. Things seemed to be happening now almost at the speed of light. My own view was that we should set up home in Suffolk, for Pam's family ties were there and I felt that in any case whilst Overdale suited me, it might not be right for Pam. The plan was that I would put Overdale on the market and we would look for a house in Suffolk. Subject to the sale of Overdale and finding the right house, Pam would then put her house up for letting. We took a flexible approach to the date of the wedding for there were many things which would influence this.

My first action was to take steps to put Overdale on the market and I therefore reluctantly left Pam and returned to Shipton Oliffe on 30th October with the intention of returning to Glemsford as soon as possible. Pam was committed to her job but after some discussion she decided to give notice to terminate it. There were some regrets in her mind about this but I said that I would not want her to go on working when we were married. It did not seem right to me that she would have to follow the discipline of a job whilst I stayed at home and did exactly as I liked.

As I drove home I was in the highest of spirits even though I was going to take the first steps in ending my connections with Overdale and the Cotswolds. I had now been gripped by something far bigger and more important than my Overdale adventure. In any case the story was by no means ended. Putting it on the market was only the first step in what became a long running saga, enlivened by one or two adventures and a great deal of fun which, this time, Pam had a share in.

The obvious person to handle the sale of Overdale was the one who sold it to me. There were many good reasons for this, chief amongst which was that I liked him as a person. He was also highly professional. He had visited Overdale in September at my request to undertake a valuation for insurance purposes and had put an insurance value of £70,000 on the property. He also gave me his opinion of the market value. He thought a figure of £65,000 would be realistic. As I had paid £44,000 for it, this was a

Transformation

remarkable appreciation. Some part was accounted for by a general rise in property values but much of it was due to the improvements which I had made to it. He had congratulated me at the time on the transformation that had taken place. He had known it in its least appealing state.

I made an appointment and visited him at his office in Cheltenham. He was delighted to learn the good news of our forthcoming marriage and offered his warmest congratulations and good wishes for the future. He was once again living up to my view of him as a true gentleman and he entered into the whole spirit of the new developments. I knew that the sale was in absolutely the best possible hands. He believed the property would sell and he had confidence that his valuation was about right. He did warn me that as winter was almost upon us, enquiries might be slow in coming, the market being somewhat sluggish at that time. On 7th November he wrote to say that Overdale was now on the market at £67,500. We had agreed that he would hold the key and would only allow inspection to take place when I was at home or, in my absence, in his company.

It now became a matter of urgency for me to complete some of the jobs which I had left and had not been urgent before. I drew up a list in priority order of the jobs which needed doing, all of which were well within my capability, on the basis of those tasks which would add to the attractiveness of the interior. There were one or two areas where some plastering was needed and several places where some small repairs to woodwork were essential. These and other places would require a coat of paint and I worked on them with speed and enthusiasm. My level of motivation was very high indeed and this enabled me to work long hours with hardly any sign of fatigue. I concentrated on the inside for we were now in November and the garden ceased to need so much attention.

There were one or two places in the ceilings on the ground floor which were badly cracked and these received early attention. To the amateur there is always a problem with a ceiling, as to how much plaster should be hacked off before replastering. I discovered that the best method was to remove the plaster which came away easily but no more. The gap could then be filled and this would have the effect of securing the plaster on the edge which I would describe as the *grey* areas. My technique was to work with a fairly stiff plaster mix and to work round the area from the outside covering a small piece at a time. If the hole was big I would let the plaster set on the edges and proceed in stages. Only the experts can plaster ceilings taking large areas at a time. It is quite a different technique when patches on walls are being replastered. Again if the plaster mix is fairly stiff the filling is not too difficult. One can always splash the plaster with water after application, to enable a smooth finish to be obtained. In the case of Overdale the plastering of the walls was in the vernacular style and a very smooth surface was the last thing one needed, nor did it need to be level. The secret was to follow the existing contours, no matter how uneven. The largest of the plastering jobs to be done was around the bedroom window where the lintel replacement had taken place and here again a stage-by-stage approach was needed. Within a few days this part of the programme was complete and drying out would have to take place before the new areas of plaster could be painted.

The painting of the doors was next on the list. Many of these were coloured cream and needed undercoat and gloss but the results were immediate and made a noticeable impact on the appearance of the rooms. In the dining room the doors were covered with a nondescript brown stain. After scanning a colour chart I decided that the ideal would be a chestnut brown gloss which claimed to be a 'one coat only' paint. No undercoat was needed (so the tin boasted) and in my case this turned out to be quite true. I am not sure that if I had been covering white paint the claim would have been valid.

Having been away from Pam for a week I decided to leave things as they were and return to Suffolk for a few days. Pam was busy making visits to apprentices and I travelled with her on her days out during that week. This was like a mini holiday for me and allowed me to see more of Suffolk than hitherto. I had travelled round it often when at work in the region but I would always be going somewhere specific and usually in a hurry. Being driven was most pleasant and I discovered (which I already knew) that it was a beautiful place; a gently undulating landscape dotted with fine timber buildings of considerable age and of all shapes and sizes, displaying a rich array of pastel colours. I had to admit to Pam that it was nearly as nice as the Cotswolds. Her view was that it was nicer than the Cotswolds and this confirmed my opinion that we ought to find our home in Suffolk.

We were now in the unusual situation of having several lines of action we could take, two of which would have been acceptable in the short term. We could live at Glemsford, we could live at Overdale or we could find a house in Suffolk. The latter would only be possible when the sale of Overdale was fairly certain. I had cleared the question of a short-term bridging loan with my bank manager and so all was set for a search for a house. We had not made any decisions as to exactly where we wanted to be other than that we both agreed that a Suffolk village would be ideal. In the early stages our search was not very positive, but we consulted the estate agents' windows and the press to get some ideas about relative values. It seemed that properties in Suffolk were valued slightly lower than in the Cotswolds, but it was not easy to compare like with like.

Much depended now on what happened in the Cotswolds and the interest shown in Overdale. I was torn between being with Pam and the need to go back to Overdale and continue my work there to make it as saleable as possible. I decided to spend the period during the week at Overdale and return to Pam for the weekends. Visits from potential buyers were scarce and the one or two who came seemed to be more curious than serious. Over time one learns enough to pick out the genuine from the phoney although all who came had obtained copies of the particulars and had made appointments.

In December I had a visit from the agent who brought his wife along. I was glad of the opportunity to meet him again and to make the acquaintance of his wife. It seemed that she was somewhat interested in his description of the place and wanted to see it. She was very absorbed by what she saw and was obviously a very keen gardener. We spent some time looking round and then I made a cup of tea which was much appreciated. I took the opportunity of discussing how we might stimulate interest in Overdale and he suggested that we might take a space in the *Cotswold Life* magazine which was a monthly publication with a wide circulation. I agreed to this on the basis of shared costs and he promised to put the matter in hand. He assured me that the property would sell, but again reminded me that this was a dead time of year for house sales.

I returned to Pam and we decided to start looking seriously for a house, knowing now that from decision to occupation would be at least eight weeks and that as spring came, house prices would rise. We drove out to Lavenham on one occasion and had a snack lunch at the Angel followed by a stroll around the village. Although I had stayed there on one occasion and driven through it many times, I had not fully appreciated what an interesting place it was. Pam of course knew it well. When we got back in the car I told Pam that of all the places we knew this was the one with most appeal and I for one would like to live there. We both realised that properties were likely to be more expensive than in some other villages but nevertheless we decided to start some serious investigations. Within a few days we had obtained details of a cottage for sale in Prentice Street and made an appointment to see it. This was the first cottage anywhere which we had inspected, on the other hand it was the only one for sale in Lavenham within our price range. I believe my judgement was somewhat clouded by the excitement of finding a property in Lavenham which was affordable and I have no doubt that I influenced Pam when we both decided we would like to live there. It was owned by a single lady who had achieved some measure of fame as a yachtswoman and was in the process of getting a crew together for the round-the-world yacht race starting in 1985. This was to be the first all-woman crew to undertake this challenge, and she needed to be amongst the yachting fraternity in the Chichester Harbour. We agreed to buy the house and she hoped to give possession by 23rd January 1985. This decision now allowed us to fix a date for our wedding which was to be Saturday, 26th January. All our future decisions would be built round this date.

Christmas was fast approaching and we had decided that it would be best to be at Glemsford for Christmas where Pam could see some of her family. It soon became clear that unless we took some steps we might suddenly find ourselves with three properties on our hands, and we came up with the idea that it would make sense for Pam to let her Glemsford house on a limited tenancy basis. It was a saleable property but it seemed that at the moment, letting it to provide Pam with a source of income was right, at least for the time being. Tenants were quickly found, well-known to Pam, and she agreed that they could take up residence there on 7th January. Their need was urgent as the house they were building would be some long time before it was ready for occupation. This meant that Pam would need to come to Overdale from that date to the time we obtained possession of the Lavenham house. This presented no problems other than the dispersal of the furniture from the house by 7th January. I insisted that Pam's 2,000 books, contained in four large bookcases, should be moved to Overdale for I knew how much she valued them. In any case it would have been almost as expensive to store them in or near Lavenham. We knew of somewhere where her furniture could be stored without charge but the space was limited.

On the day before Christmas Eve we sustained a most unwelcome blow when we received a telephone call from the owner of the Lavenham cottage saying that she had decided not to sell. She had been unable to progress her plans about moving and would need to stay in Lavenham. This came as a considerable shock as we had built all our plans round the date of possession, namely 23rd January. The date of the wedding was fixed and all the invitations were out. There was nothing we could do but accept the situation and start our search for another property. We had set our minds on Lavenham and turned our attention once more to the agents. What happened next was a chance in a million. A property had just come on the market in Lavenham High Street. It was at a similar price to the other, and it was with great excitement that we got the details and made a dash for Lavenham and knocked at the door. We were welcomed by the owner (his wife was at work) who showed us round. It was a magical experience and one we shall never forget for the house was everything we could wish for. It was very old but in superb condition. It had three bedrooms and was full of exposed timbers. The carpets and curtains were included in the sale and were almost new, and at the back there was a pretty little garden. We were both captivated by it and told the owner that we wished to buy it. He said they hoped to move by early March and this was ideal from our point of view. I told him we would be going straight back to the agent and setting the purchase in motion. We could not believe our luck and we both agreed that it was more suitable than the one we first selected. We were not trying to console ourselves for it truly was a very desirable place.

Having now secured our home in Lavenham, we were able to proceed with our plans. I had booked a date for the removal of the books and bookcases to Overdale and I went ahead to receive them, returning to Glemsford the same day ready to move furniture into store on the following day.

We left Glemsford on 7th January in two cars with Pam's wardrobe and the white cat, Moby Dick. Moby had been a slight source of concern to me although I had nothing against him. As I think of him now I feel somewhat guilty that I should have had these doubts for we became great friends. My doubts arose from the well-known fact that cats are creatures which become very attached to places and here we were subjecting him to this upheaval which would be shortly followed by another.

The other question mark I had was the selfish one of wondering whether he might intervene in our plans for taking holidays and periods away from home. There was no need for these anxieties and in any case his fondness for Pam and hers for him were very real. I came to terms with the fact that I must now share responsibility for his welfare.

I had suggested that we should familiarise him with the cat basket we were using to transport him to Overdale, and in fact he did occupy it from time to time. On the morning of departure he submitted to the lid being closed and being transported to Pam's car. But from that moment on he hated every minute of the journey. He cried from Suffolk to Overdale much to Pam's distress and I felt very guilty afterwards that she had had to endure it all on her own.

On arrival at Overdale, he, quite rightly, was given top priority. I was very apprehensive lest he should be so disturbed as to escape from the confines of the house. The design of the house was such that only the kitchen opened on to the exterior. All other rooms gave access to the outside after passing through two doors. This meant that we could keep him safely from escape. In the event after an initial period of apparent depression he settled down and made no attempt to leave the house and became very much at home there. After a time we felt confident that he would not wish to escape and he had freedom to move where he wished, including out of doors. He did not venture far but this was not unusual as he was over 20 years old. His days of hunting were long passed although when the occasion demanded he could spring into action. His slow movements belied the sharpness of his natural instincts and, should another cat appear at the front door of the cottage, it would retreat at speed when Moby took up his most aggressive attitude, poised ready to spring at the intruder. I became very fond of him and he began to realise that I was a soft touch. He would sit at my feet as I read the paper and occasionally reminded me of his presence by sinking his claws into my knees. When we eventually left Overdale he accepted the change as philosophically as he had done when we moved there and enjoyed a good retirement, taking life very easy. It was thought he was 22 years old when he died, a remarkable cat, independent, resourceful, highly intelligent and extremely proud.

It was nice to be back at Overdale and to have Pam with me for we had passed through a pretty hectic period of considerable upheaval. Now we could look forward to the end of January when we would be married and onwards to March when we would move to Lavenham. Although I had grown very fond of the place and enjoyed every minute of my life there, the time comes when we need to move on and this was the time. I was embarking on a new phase of my life and moving to Suffolk was an essential part of it. I had no regrets whatsoever about the decision to go, and in the meantime there was much to do and much to enjoy until we moved.

I continued to work on the list of jobs I had set myself but now at a more leisurely pace. Pam took over the running of the house and from time to time gave me a helping hand. She enjoyed decorating and we spent a lot of time with brushes in our hands; all of it well spent as Overdale's appearance inside was much enhanced as a result. One major task I tackled was to point an exposed wall in the sitting room. Early on I had stripped the plaster (and some cement) off this wall. It all started when some plaster fell off. I took off some more which was loose and ended up with half the wall exposed displaying the Cotswold stone in all its glory. It seemed to me that the best thing was to expose the whole of the wall and let it stand as a feature. Clearing the plaster and cement from the wall was hard but eventually I finished it and had left it until this point. To complete the job and really make it attractive, pointing was necessary and in any case it needed sealing. Pointing was a long and tedious process for much of the wall was built with small stones. I worked at it in short spells, for to have tried to do it by sticking at it day after day would have been demoralising. It took several weeks in the end but the finished job was very rewarding, particularly when I fixed up two spotlights to bring it to life. I had achieved the effect I believed to be possible and my efforts were amply rewarded. All those who came to view the house commented on the wall and this was very gratifying.

Time was flying by and although we had not yet found a buyer for Overdale, our wedding day was fixed and some hundred people had responded positively to our invitation. We had sent a letter by way of invitation, saying that if anyone thought of giving us a present it should be limited to £5 and preferably in money. Our aim was to buy a new washing machine for our new home which we needed. All our guests thought this was an excellent idea and we were able to buy the machine. We were anxious that people should not spend more than a minimum amount and it worked to the satisfaction of all concerned.

We held a wonderful party at the Swan in Lavenham and everyone including the bride and groom enjoyed it immensely. We returned to Overdale the day after the wedding and settled down to our new life together, determined now to take life somewhat easier than we had been doing over the many weeks before. There was no shortage of things to do but they could be done when we felt like it. They would be optional extras rather than essential jobs, for Overdale was now at its best, warm, bright and very comfortable. Just right for viewing by any prospective buyer – how could they resist it?

There was always considerable excitement when we got a call from the agent to ask whether it was convenient for a client to visit and although the house was always reasonably tidy, there would be things to be done to present it in pristine condition. There were always things to put away in their respective places and some dusting to be done, and on occasions when visitors arrived unannounced and wanted a look (having seen the advertising board outside) a certain amount of scrambling about went on for we never turned anyone away. I would keep them talking in the sitting room whilst Pam would dash round the house making it all tidy. On one particular occasion Pam stuffed my pullover under the grill in panic and was reminded of her action the next time she switched on the grill to prepare the evening meal (end of pullover).

The most amusing encounter was with the tycoon who was accompanied by his architect. I happened to be working in the garden at the time. Pam had met them at the front door and shown them round the ground floor with the intention of introducing them to me. Before this could happen, the tycoon had taken over the whole situation and said they would just go outside and do some measuring up. He came out of the back door completely ignoring me and with his architect proceeded to measure up with a view to building an extension. I stood witnessing all this saying nothing and he completely ignored my presence. After a while I tentatively approached them suggesting that the planning authority might not allow such a development. He shot me down in flames and I retreated to my post in the garden. He obviously thought I was the gardener and I thought I had better not shatter his illusions. Needless to say, we heard no more of him.

There was a lady, her daughter and son-in-law with a strong urban accent who wanted to keep sheep. She was very put out when she saw the extent of the land available for she felt she had been misled. I got the feeling that her problem was one of lack of reading skills.

A blonde girl of about nineteen came accompanied by her gangling, fair-haired, pony-tailed young man and a small dark girl. They entered exuding great confidence, saying that they were living in a two roomed flat in Cheltenham and were hankering after a new life in the countryside. We had grave doubts about their ability to find any money, let alone £65,000. There was some hint that Daddy might help, but we heard no more.

The tall, cultured man who had seen the announcement in *Cotswold Life* was just passing and thought he would have a look. He was very patronising, and made it very clear that he was looking for something much grander than Overdale. I drew back from saying that if that was the case it was a pity that he had wasted so much of our valuable time.

One Sunday morning towards the end of February we were having a pre-lunch drink when I spotted a young couple walking slowly along the road in front of the cottage and glancing surreptitiously at it. I watched them turn on their way back to their car and realised that they were interested in the house. I took the initiative and went outside to have a word with them. They were in fact searching for a house to buy and seeing our sign had stopped to look. I invited them to look round but they said as it was so close to lunchtime it might be better to come back in the afternoon if we agreed. On their return I introduced them to Pam and then gave them the full history of the last 12 months and what had been done. We told them why we were leaving and gave them some details of the surrounding area. We then had a thorough tour of the property inside and out and it was becoming clear as we went that they had taken a liking to Overdale. The lady was entranced by all she saw for she had a great capacity for showing her feelings. They were a most charming couple and extremely polite, a quality which is regrettably rare. They were by far the nicest people out of all the ones viewing the place. We all quickly became at ease with each other and when they said they would like to buy Overdale I could hardly conceal my delight. Apart from everything else I knew we should not find nicer people to become the new owners. We agreed a price subject to a satifsactory survey being undertaken and I accepted this arrangement. They also said that they were in no great hurry to take up occupation and for us this was an added advantage. I mentioned that they were a number of items I wanted to sell, such as the Mountfield mower, a substantial ladder and other gardening equipment and they were happy to buy these.

They took their leave and thanked us for our helpfulness and it was clear that they were just as pleased as we were with the happenings of the last two hours. This was a red letter day for us and we celebrated with a drink, knowing that unless the survey revealed any horrors, which we were positive it would not, we had a buyer for Overdale, and everything would now fit into place.

The surveyor came and spent several hours carrying out the most careful survey of the cottage and its environs which included a climb into the roof space. On 4th March we had word that the sale would proceed subject to contract and that the purchasers hoped to complete by 30th April.

Pickford's removal van arrived at Overdale on the morning of 30th April. The agreement was they they would do all the necessary packing, and the four men who arrived with the van made very short work of clearing the cottage. The van pulled away before lunchtime and after cleaning through the house with the vacuum cleaner, we too were ready to leave. Our neighbours came to say goodbye, and so did Paul who had been so much a part of the adventure which had now closed. I took the opportunity of thanking him for his considerable effort and for his robust support.

This brief chapter in my life had now ended and a new one was beginning. It had been a very full and eventful period and one which I shall never forget and certainly never regret. Following one's first instincts is often the right thing to do. In this case it turned out to be so.